Lincoln Christian

Contents

Preface

For a number of years I have had an interest in oral tradition and related problems, although not as a specialist. Since 1968, I have been fortunate enough to receive some grants to support my research in this area. Support came from the Humanities Research Fund of McGill University from 1968 to 1970. More directly associated with this present work were two grants from Canada Council, in 1971-72 for a research leave and in 1972-73 for a research assistant. The title of the research project was "Oral Tradition and the Literature of Ancient Israel," two elements of which were oral prose transmission and structural analysis. I would like to express my gratitude for all this assistance.

Thanks are also due those who were research assistants for longer or shorter periods during these years: Murray Henderson, Alan Hayes, Kenneth MacQueen, Erin Malloy, and Matthias Benfey.

This monograph had been submitted before I was able to see Brevard Childs' commentary on Exodus, and so only limited use of it could be made while making a few final revisions. John Van Seters' book, *Abraham in History and Tradition*, arrived when I was part way through these final revisions. Unfortunately, I had to restrict myself to a few comments in order to give some indication of my initial response to his views. They touch closely on much that is presented here.

Robert C. Culley
Montreal, September 1975

Introduction

The word "studies" in the title of this work indicates that the three parts into which it is divided have a measure of independence in the sense that each part is limited in scope and treats a restricted amount of material. Part I considers the nature of oral prose by examining four field studies. Part II reviews a selection of parallel narratives, some of the so-called doublets of the Hebrew Bible. Part III brings together a small group of stories containing a miraculous happening in order to explore structures shared by these stories.

On the other hand, these three parts are related to each other in a number of ways so that bringing them together in one monograph is not only appropriate but useful. In the first place, a movement from an interest in oral tradition to an interest in structure has been a natural one in scholarship. Folklorists studying oral narratives have moved quite easily and naturally to questions of structure (see, for example, Maranda and Köngäs Maranda, 1971). Then too, there may be some advantage in approaching the difficult problems of structure in Hebrew narrative, an ancient body of traditional material, by using as a starting point studies of people who actually construct stories, oral narrators who create traditional narratives anew in each performance. For example, Erhard Güttgemanns, who is deeply interested in the structural analysis of biblical texts, has made the claim that the understanding of the concept "text" gained from the study of oral literature is helpful in developing the notions of structure and text in his generative poetics approach (1973:3). Finally, it was interesting to discover that oral tradition, doublets, and structure were among the topics receiving considerable attention in John Van Seters' book, *Abraham in History and Tradition* (1975). These are the topics of the three parts of this present work, although Van Seters has taken a different tack, especially in the treatment of structure.

While Part III is more explicitly focused on the question of the structure of texts, the concern with structure is present throughout and follows a logical progression. The study of oral prose in the first part throws out clues that are pursued in the second and third parts. The second part follows up the question of oral style in biblical texts but at the same time develops the notion of structure which is taken up in the third part.

Finally, running through the whole is a constant exploration of repeated patterns of different kinds at different levels of the text. On the one hand, there is the question of variation in oral tradition. This is pursued in biblical texts by considering the problem of parallel segments of narrative as oral or written variants. On the other hand, the miracle stories can be seen as variants of patterns at a more abstract or deeper level of the text.

Part I

Oral Transmission of Prose

The approach to the question of the structure of narrative is initiated indirectly by the consideration of another question: the nature of the transmission of oral prose. What is known about how prose works are created and transmitted in oral tradition? To answer this question it was decided to look for field studies in which careful examinations have been made of the process of oral tradition in specific groups. True, this sort of information can only provide starting points, in that one must still decide how to move from the specific statements in particular field studies to more general statements which might be regarded as universally applicable. Nevertheless, even a modest sampling of reports about oral transmission of prose could show what is possible in this kind of transmission, and might also indicate what is probable. In other words, the task is one of mapping out the possibilities, or what we know can happen in oral transmission of prose, and then indicating the probabilities, or what seems to happen frequently. The degree of success achieved in such an undertaking depends directly on the number and nature of field studies available. Clearly, any subsequent application of results gained to biblical material must be a second and separate step. After the field studies have been examined and before this second step is begun, one must consider to what extent it is legitimate and relevant to use information gained from field studies to make statements about biblical texts.

Of course, some general information about oral tradition, both poetry and prose, has been available for some time and consequently some general statements can be made about the range of possibilities (Culley, 1963). For example it is known that poems and stories can be passed on in a fixed form. It appears, however, that transmission can also be accomplished in an unfixed form in which the performer presents a different version

1

of a given traditional story or poem in each performance. This last phenomenon is held to be very common in the transmission of both prose and poetry.

Before moving on to the specific problem of the transmission of oral prose, some further general comments can be made about oral tradition on the basis of two general studies, one dealing with European tradition and one dealing with African tradition.

The first of these is an article, "Principles of Oral Transmission of Folk Culture," by the Hungarian folklorist, Gyula Ortutay (Ortutay, 1959). While this article aims at stating a few general principles, it is based to a large extent on the author's own field experience, although reference is made to the work of other scholars as well. In describing what goes on in transmission of oral tradition, Ortutay sees change as a very frequent characteristic. He argues that

> even the meaning of such words as *creation, transmission,*
> *retelling, resinging* forms an almost inextricable tangle.
> Retelling nearly always involves a change; it is an act of
> variation which may be creative at the same time, while — in
> its later, final stages — oral transmission comes to be
> equivalent to deterioration, to a process of stuttering
> forgetfulness. (180)

Ortutay distinguishes three kinds of change, each of which he discusses in some detail. There is a process of deterioration and corruption, a process of creation and embellishment, and a process which he calls "affinity." Change is by no means all in the direction of disintegration. Change can be a positive tendency.

> We are convinced that the decisive characteristic of re-creative
> oral transmission is not simple preservation but a tendency
> towards embellishment and enrichment. (207)

The third type of change, affinity, has to do with how new types and forms are created through attraction of similar types, motifs, and formal elements. This last process, Ortutay claims, needs further examination and study.

The other general study to be referred to is a recent book by Ruth Finnegan, *Oral Literature in Africa* (Finnegan, 1970). This work is particularly interesting because it deals with oral tradition in an area other than Europe, since so much of the field work on oral tradition has been European. Finnegan's book is an attempt to bring together and review the scholarly material on oral literature in various parts of Africa. Her own field work in Africa will be considered at a later point.

In speaking of composition and transmission, Finnegan indicates the wide range of possibilities reflected in reports on African oral literature. She sums up the situation this way:

> It is clear that the process is by no means the same in all non-literate cultures or all types of oral literature, and between the extremes of totally new creation and memorized reproduction of set pieces there is scope for many different theories and practices of composition. (7f.)

Yet, having admitted the range of possibilities which exist, Finnegan is struck by the frequency of change during transmission and so she lists "verbal variability" as a notable characteristic of oral literature. The claim is made that, even though the opportunity of a narrator to be creative may vary, "there is almost always some opportunity for 'composition'" (9). Finally, in Finnegan's discussion of prose materials, the following comments can be found:

> Contrary to the assumptions of many writers, the likelihood of stories having been handed down from generation to generation in a word-perfect form is in practice very remote. . . . one of the main characteristics of oral literature is its verbal flexibility. . . . (319)

Thus both Ortutay and Finnegan regard variation due to creative change as a major feature of oral literature. These observations are consistent with other general information available on oral tradition referred to at the start.

FOUR FIELD STUDIES ON ORAL PROSE

Now, it is time to focus more sharply on the question of the way in which oral prose is composed and transmitted. Since people have been collecting folktales, legends and other kinds of oral prose for some time, especially in Europe, a great deal has been written about the material collected, and many comments on various aspects of transmission are probably available. The problem here is to choose the most suitable material. It was decided to look for recent field studies which had paid considerable attention to testing what happened to stories as they were repeated not only by the same narrator but by other narrators as well. Four studies of this type were selected, and, it must be said, there were not many studies of this sort to choose from. The four selected came from different parts of the world.

1. Crowley

The first study is *I Could Talk Old-Story Good: Creativity in Bahamian Folklore* by Daniel J. Crowley (Crowley, 1966). This book grew out of an investigation of prose stories in an oral tradition still flourishing in the villages of the Bahama Islands which stretch from Florida to Haiti. These stories were told in the evenings for entertainment. During the course of an evening several storytellers might participate for long or short periods. Crowley describes the folklore of these Islands as that of "illiterates in a literate society, rather than non-literates in an isolated exotic society" (3). In his opinion, the kind of narration studied is nowhere near a period of decline but on the contrary shows signs of being able to thrive for some time to come.

His study arose from the question of the creative role of the narrator of traditional tales. Crowley puts his purpose this way:

> This study was made in order to discover, by minute examination of a body of tales, exactly what makes up its "tradition," how and by whom it is transmitted, and where, when, why, how, and by how much it is varied. . . . Its ultimate goal is a cross-culturally valid description of the nature of aesthetic creativity in its relationship to tradition. (3)

With this aim in mind, Crowley took considerable pains to do his collecting carefully and systematically. For example, a tape recorder was used to capture the narration as it was performed before an audience. Then, too, narrators were often asked to repeat tales after an interval so that it would be possible to compare material at different points in time. Crowley was also able to draw on some texts collected by others over the past seventy years. This material added further checks on what happened to stories over a span of repeated narration.

The type of story investigated was a variety of traditional folktale known as "old-stories." Crowley characterizes these stories this way:

> Only traditional motifs may be used in an old-story, plus a few "original" motifs totally in the spirit of the tradition. . . . Old-stories also have a definite structural arrangement capable of extensive variation, but only rarely overlapping another traditional Bahamian form. (15)

The simplest way to convey the kind of story spoken of here is to mention some of the standard characters each of whom may play different roles from story to story. B'Rabby is the trickster and B'Booky his stupid foil. B'Jack is a clever boy hero. B'Devil is a kind of trickster who is always overcome by the hero. Miss Different is the devil's shrewish wife or secretary (28ff.). There is also a whole cast of animal characters.

In addition to standard characters, there are other stock elements which can be mentioned. These include several traditional opening and closing formulas as well as traditional stylistic devices and motifs. It is worth noting that the similarity of this Bahamian tradition to other New World traditions leads Crowley to suggest that Africa is the most likely common place of origin.

According to Crowley, the Bahamian folktale is "a series of traditional motifs arranged in a more or less logical pattern of action" (40). The arrangement varies with the telling since the stories are not repeated exactly with each retelling. In Crowley's view, the motifs are a key element of traditional material used by the narrator to build his tale each time it is retold. In his use of the term "motif," Crowley claims to be following Stith Thompson's widely known definition which says that a motif is "the smallest element in a tale having the power to persist in tradition," including such things as characters, objects, and incidents. In subsequent discussion, however, Crowley appears to identify motif with incident so that when he says that stories may have from two to ten motifs he means that they may be constructed of anywhere from two to ten incidents (40ff.). In his detailed analysis of the use of motifs in constructing stories, he limits himself for reasons of method to a particular set of trickster tales. A remarkable result of this investigation of the use of motifs or incidents is "the almost total lack of patterning in the sequence of motif occurrence, and the free combining and recombining of motifs that make a new story at each retelling" (42). This observation leads to problems when it comes to talking about a "story" or "tale type" since so much freedom with regard to rearrangement of motifs, and thus of story structure, is possible. On the other hand, varying the motifs in a story "is the major means by which a narrator produces significantly different variants" (44).

Finally, two observations from Crowley's conclusions may be noted by way of summary. The Bahamian old-stories have been found to be organized around the principle of multiple internal variability, with a wide range of traditional materials, both structural and thematic, from which the narrator makes up his tale. The skilled narrator combines and recombines them each time he tells a story, so that each tale is new each time it is told (135). The last paragraph of Crowley's monograph deserves to be quoted in full.

> A Bahamian folktale may be likened to a kaleidoscope with its finite number of bits of colored glass representing the traditional and original motifs and style elements of the narrators; the kaleidoscopic mirrors representing the tradition that integrates the scattered pieces into a design, and the hand of the person who shakes the kaleidoscope being the half-conscious, half-unconscious creativity of the storyteller. As the

kaleidoscope produces a new and unique design at each
shaking, so the Bahamian folktale is a new and unique story at
each retelling. (141)

The situation described by Crowley fits the general picture of
oral tradition set out at the start and illustrated by references to
Ortutay and Finnegan. But there is a new factor which needs to be
emphasized and kept in mind. While Crowley speaks of various
traditional materials which are at the narrator's disposal, it seems
that the crucial stock element in building tales is the motif which
Crowley appears to equate in his analysis with incident. Strangely
enough, stock incidents are seldom shaped into larger story
patterns or plots, so that stories are simply combinations of a
number of stock incidents.

2. Finnegan
    The second study is *Limba Stories and Story-Telling* by Ruth
Finnegan (Finnegan, 1967). The Limba are rice farmers in
northern Sierra Leone. Although they do not themselves classify
their stories into different types, Finnegan employs a threefold
classification for convenience in handling the material. First,
there are stories about people, these being the most common and
most elaborate. They have a number of stock leading figures.
Then, there are stories about the god Kanu and origins. Last, there
are stories about animals. Here, too, a few standard leading
figures appear frequently.

    In using this threefold classification, Finnegan has avoided
current folklore terminology. Her main reason is the fact
mentioned above that the Limba themselves recognize only one
general class of story within which they make no distinctions or
sub-classes. The validity of this approach need not be pursued
here. An additional reason for her decision not to make
classifications of types of stories beyond those already mentioned
is the fluid nature of the stories. The narrator, the audience, and
the occasion have a great deal to do with what a story is like. She
claims that

> . . . all stories, to a greater or lesser degree according to
> circumstances, can contain some or all of several
> elements — moralizing and generalization; explanation;
> comparison, whether implicit or stated as an explicit dilemma;
> and, finally, an intention to amuse and entertain by an
> interesting plot, a shocking episode or character, and a vivid
> style and delivery. (31)

Limba stories are usually told during the evening in informal
groups or gatherings. Narrators tell stories in turns. Even though
anyone is able to tell stories, some narrators are recognized as
better than others. Most of the stories used as a basis for analysis
were recorded on tape or taken down by dictation with an
audience present. On the basis of the experience of collecting the
texts and a subsequent study of them, Finnegan is prepared to
make some general statements about the nature of story-telling
among the Limba.

> There is no 'received' or correct text of any traditional story.
> Limba story-telling is a living art and the traditional themes
> and motifs find their realization in the actual performance,
> embellished on each separate occasion with differing dramatic
> devices, emphases, and wording, or with episodes or references
> peculiar to the occasion. Even the 'same' story told by the same
> story-teller may vary from narration to narration, in wording
> as well as enactment. (vii)

The balance of stability and novelty is described by the author this
way:

> There is a common fund of plots, stock openings and
> conclusions, actions and characters, but . . . the exact nature of
> the story itself in each case depends on the individual occasion
> and individual narrator. (91)

In discussing the traditional elements used by narrators to
construct their traditional stories, Finnegan restricts herself to
listing a few of the common elements (89). But she does not go a
step further to ask whether some of these elements might be more
fundamental or important to story building than others. Among
the traditional elements mentioned are the openings and closings
of stories. These take a standard form and are employed very

frequently. Other traditional elements have to do with the structure of the stories. Finnegan claims that constructing stories by means of a string of parallel, that is, the repetition of similar, episodes is an important characteristic of Limba stories.

> In a general way, each story, whatever its main topic, tends to move through a series of parallel actions which provide the main structure of the story. (89)

It is also quite common to have such parallel episodes marked off by the interjection of songs. The beginning of an episode frequently contains phrases indicating time or statements having verbs of motion. Similarly, the ending of an episode has characteristic markers.

In speaking of the structure of the story, Finnegan notes that there are two ways in which a narrator can expand or compress a story. The first is by increasing or decreasing the number of parallel or repeated incidents. The second is by elaboration. As Finnegan puts it:

> . . . there is what might be called a common fund of standard events, turns, or runs which occur in many stories, not so much as part of the basic plot or form as a potential elaboration of it. These include such common episodes as . . . the trapping of an enemy up a tree . . . a girl running away from a man who may marry her if he can catch her . . . someone dying, then being revived by leaf-medicine . . . . (90)

There are also smaller elements, such as descriptions of actions like someone sharpening a sword which serve as traditional elaborations. She sums up with this statement.

> All these, and many other short events or turns, occur and recur in different contexts in many of the stories, elaborating or embroidering the basic structures of the tale. (90)

Finally, a few comments may be added which reflect how the Limba themselves understood their storytelling and to what degree they were conscious of the process. On the one hand, they seem to be aware of a definite contribution by the storyteller (90). Finnegan mentions that a storyteller may indicate that he has been thinking over a story for a day or a few days before he tells it. Or, a narrator may say that he has contributed something of his own or that he has told the story in his own way. On the other hand, Finnegan is convinced that the narrators are fully aware of the fact that the stories are traditional tales which they have heard from others. From the point of view of an investigator, she can remark that "there is continual recreation or improvisation and yet this takes place within the framework of traditional style and theme" (102). She points out, however, that the Limba indicate much the same thing when they say that the narrator is "taught by the dead and his own heart" (102).

The kind of transmission process described by Finnegan for the Limba is very much like that described by Crowley for the Bahamians. Finnegan points out the role traditional elements have in building and elaborating stories but, while mentioning several kinds of traditional elements used, she does not define these items very specifically nor does she try to estimate the relative importances of these items in building stories. The Limba tradition would appear to be different from the Bahamian tradition in that Finnegan speaks of plot outlines, not found by Crowley, which can be elaborated or compressed. Nevertheless, standard episodes or incidents are one of the elements which, according to Finnegan, are used to expand and elaborate basic plots.

3. Dégh

The third field study to be considered is a work by Linda Dégh, *Folktales and Society* (Dégh, 1969). The first few sentences of her preface contain a very clear statement of the aim of the book.

> This book presents an investigation of storytelling by the correlation of oral folk narratives, their creators and performers, and the participant audience as a complex whole in the expression of culture. Choosing a transplanted Bucovina Szekler community now residing in the village of Kakasd (County Tolna, Hungary) as a point of departure, I have aimed at reaching general conclusions about the social role and cultural values of narration. This study of the Kakasd people emphasizes the interaction of personality and community in oral creation. (vii)

The research involved twelve field trips between 1948 and 1960. The telling of tales was very much alive in the community during this period. Almost all could tell traditional tales, but the stories collected and studied came from the best narrators whose worth was readily recognized by those who made up their audience.

Dégh points out that in communities like the one studied two systems of narrating have emerged (82). In the one system, a number of persons would narrate one after the other in any given storytelling session. This would appear to describe the situation which applied in the field studies by Crowley and Finnegan already discussed above. This kind of storytelling situation leads generally to shorter tales. In the other, it is the single, outstanding narrator who fills the spotlight and who therefore must be prepared to continue a tale for the whole evening, or perhaps for several evenings. Dégh's investigation concentrates on outstanding storytellers.

As have a number of folklorists before her, Dégh points out another distinction that can be made with regard to narrators. Narrators can be classified according to the way they handle traditional material. This can lead to a large number of categories. Dégh mentions two types: the creative narrator and passive preserver.

> The special gift of any storyteller consists in his being able to shape a tale. He is able not only to narrate well, however, but to keep in his memory a great number of tales from the traditional supply — more than the average person could retain, and he constantly reworks them in accordance with his own artistic talents. In this he differs from — and stands head and shoulders above — the simple carriers, the passive preservers of tradition, and the type of storyteller who serves merely as a mediator of tales. (171-72)

The passive bearers nevertheless serve an important function in that they transmit the basic matter of the tale. From this basic material the gifted storyteller can produce his outstanding performances.

Dégh's observations corroborate the observations of other investigators before her: the storyteller shapes the story afresh in each performance. Their stories are not retained in a fixed form. Strangely enough, the narrators themselves have insisted when asked that their tales do not change. Dégh refers to one of Ortutay's storytellers who insisted that to change these stories learned from the past would be unthinkable. Yet, recordings taken twenty years apart showed considerable change (167). Similarly, when confronted by the claim that he had told a story differently, one of Dégh's narrators suggested that the error must be with the collector and continued to insist that he had told the story in question word for word as he had before (180).

One of the skills a good narrator must develop is the ability to lengthen or shorten tales. This is closely related to the fact that narration occurs before an audience. If the narrator perceives that his audience is not attentive, then he may choose to cut his tale short and finish up quickly, but, if he senses a good response, he may be encouraged to go on for one evening or more (83, 113). This ability to shorten or lengthen a performance is well known from the observation of poetic as well as prose traditions. Dégh remarks in this connection that "the conscious act of composition included in arbitrary lengthening is possible because the folktale is composed of independent, well-rounded episodes" (83). Yet, this is only one element involved in the construction of traditional tales. Dégh notes where some of the "possibilities for the reshaping" of tales by a narrator can be found:

> They can occur in the tale structure (the possibilities for combination of motifs are infinite) or in the individual shaping, in the way the narrator actualizes the tale (whether he makes the recital epic, dramatic, or lyrical, satirical, fantastic, sentimental, or rational), and they depend on whether his manner of narrating aims at breadth, length, detail, precision, or density of content. (172)

Dégh's description of how narratives are constructed is not as explicit as one might have hoped. She seems to recognize that there are some key building blocks, as indicated in the foregoing paragraph, where her comments suggest that the episode plays a central role. On the whole, however, references to elements used in constructing tales are couched in very general terms. An example is the comment that the "tale is altered mostly by the change in motifs" (179). In view of the fact, already mentioned in the discussion of Crowley's work, that "motif" is a vague term indeed, it would have been helpful to have a more precise analysis of the nature and role of the different kinds of motifs used in narrative building, especially with regard to what Dégh calls episodes.

Some comments in another book, a collection of Hungarian folktales edited and provided with an introduction and notes by Dégh, may shed a bit more light on the matter (Dégh, 1965a). Here Dégh explains that the tales have a framework much like the standard tale "types" found in folklore indices. Into this framework are fitted episodes, motifs, and sometimes even tale types which have been subordinated to the role of episodes (xxx-xxxi). The use of a framework indicates that these tales are more than a simple combination of motifs like the Bahamian stories of Crowley's investigation.

4. Scheub

The last of the four studies consists of the work of Harold Scheub, a very detailed analysis of a story type called the *ntsomi* from the Xhosa of southern Africa. Scheub's main study is a dissertation, "The *Ntsomi*: A Xhosa Performing Art," submitted to the University of Wisconsin in 1969. The dissertation has not been published but some articles based on it have appeared (1970, 1971, and 1972). This study of the *ntsomi* came from material collected in the course of a field trip lasting several months in 1967-68 during which well over two thousand *ntsomi* performances were recorded on tape in various parts of Transkei. A selection of 114 texts, mostly from a single district, were chosen for analysis in the dissertation. All the texts appear in full in an English translation and almost half have the original Xhosa as well.

Scheub prefers to avoid the use of the term "text" when referring to the items he recorded because his contention is that the objects of his study are dramatic performances in which the use of gesture and voice play significant roles. Thus, instead of speaking of an *ntsomi* text, he uses terms like "*ntsomi*-image,"

"*ntsomi*-performance," and "*nstomi*-production." The term
"image" is used very frequently, and by this is meant the dramatic
performance, the finished production (1969:17). At one point,
however, Scheub resorts to more familiar language describing the
nstomi as a "fabulous story, unbelievable, a fairy tale, a seemingly
insignificant piece of fantasy, endlessly repetitious" (1970:119)
and goes on to remark that one meets in these stories talking
animals, birds, and monsters. It would seem, then, that the stories
Scheub presents are something like the folktales in the field
studies just considered.

The *ntsomi* is normally performed by a woman. The
performances occur before members of the family, neighbors and
friends sometimes being present also. According to Scheub, the
primary purpose of such performances is for private
entertainment. The stories are traditional and well known, yet the
artists do not memorize fixed texts. There are certain traditional
elements which the artist knows and works with. These provide
stability. On the other hand, the artist is free to select and choose,
expanding and contracting the story at will, all of which indicates
a good measure of flexibility. In speaking of the performance of
these stories, Scheub offers the following observations:

> This constant process of arrangement and rearrangement of
> details and episodes is a part of the creative process and is
> deeply involved in the aesthetics of *ntsomi*-production. The
> artist has inherited kaleidoscopic possibilities for *ntsomi*-
> creation, and she is free within the limits of the thematic-image,
> and within the bounds of logic and cohesiveness, to deal with
> them as she chooses. (1969:192)

Scheub has made considerable effort to describe in some detail
the process involved in *ntsomi*-performances. In order to do this,
he has created his own technical vocabulary. He did this largely
because he is moving into a new area, the technical description of
the process of oral prose composition during a performance, and
there was no ready-made vocabulary at hand among students of
oral prose. Scheub did not mention the work of Albert B. Lord on
oral composition in traditional oral narrative poetry (1960) but

refers to it in an article (1970:145) where he still asserts the need for new terminology.

The broadest term is "image" which, as pointed out above, is used to refer to a dramatic performance. Scheub speaks of images where some others might speak of texts. An image, or the text of a performance, is made up of one or more elements which Scheub calls "core-images." Each core-image has a nucleus called a "core-cliché." A core-cliché is normally a saying, song, or chant related to the subject matter of the core-image. Core-clichés may be repeated several times during a performance of a given story. In trying to account for the creative process by which the artist is able to produce a narrative during a performance using traditional elements, Scheub suggests that the core-clichés are the key elements in remembering the traditional stories in that they call to mind the the core-images, the traditional elements out of which the stories are built by the narrator. In Scheub's view, the core-clichés (songs, chants, and sayings) are the most stable elements in the tradition and easily remembered, "the most reliable cues in the process of recalling the core images" (1969:188). Scheub sums it up this way:

> Almost all such images contain a cliché which is basic to its internal structure and which becomes the core of repeated actions. When a song, chant or saying is recalled, also recalled are allied and supporting details and episodes, i.e., the entire core-image. (188)

While the process of remembering traditional elements may work this way, what one meets in the *ntsomi* texts which Scheub has provided are realized core-images in a narrative form so that he can provide for each core-image what he calls a "core-plot," a summary of the essential narrative action of the several realizations of the core-image in the collected performances. In the 114 texts which form the basis of Scheub's study, he is able to identify seventy-eight core-images which recur in these texts. Each realization of a given core-image appears in different wording, and some examples may be much longer and more detailed than others. Nevertheless, all the realizations of a core-image are similar enough so that a summary core-plot can be stated which is valid for all examples of the core-image. Thus, it would appear that the core-images, each involving a core-plot with one or more episodes, are when realized in the *ntsomi* texts traditional building blocks of traditional stories and are consequently similar to the phenomenon discussed in the field studies of Crowley, Finnegan, and Dégh, referred to variously as motifs, stock scenes, and episodes. It is worth noting that Scheub remarks that the plot-cores are among the first things youthful artists learn (1969:60).

The general process of narration during performance described by Scheub sounds much like that met in the other field studies. Traditional texts were not memorized but performed in such a way that there was both stability and flexibility. Scheub notes that the artist who performs the *ntsomi* has two central roles:

> . . . that of medium, externalizing the core-images of the past, and that of the artist, imaginatively selecting, controlling and arranging the materials and sources of the past and present, and giving them new life and freshness. (1969:180)

This, then, finishes the review of the four field studies. To what extent can an answer be made to the question posed at the start: what do we know about how prose is actually created and transmitted in oral tradition? It is already clear that this question can be answered only in very limited ways. The number of field studies available is small. Even these are not uniform in their description of the process in the sense that there was a varying degree of precision and completeness of description when it came to setting out the devices of composition. This is not a criticism of the studies. The authors had different approaches and interests. Broadly speaking, all the field studies described the oral composition of prose in similar terms. Traditional stories were passed on in an unfixed form in which a loyalty to tradition, and therefore a certain stability, was combined with a creative retelling, and therefore a certain flexibility. All four studies mentioned traditional elements used by narrators to construct their stories during performance. Among the traditional elements used by narrators, it was fairly clear that the stock incident or episode was a very important element. In Crowley's study, it seemed that the stock incident was a key item in building tales, especially since there did not seem to be much use of plot outlines. In Finnegan's study, stock incidents and episodes were certainly an important device used to fill plot outlines. Perhaps more clearly than Finnegan, Dégh points to the stock episode as a vital factor in building tales by filling plot outlines. Dégh adds the interesting point that some plot outlines of stories can also serve as episodes in other stories. Finally, Scheub spoke of core-images which could be summarized in core-plots, segments of narration with one or more episodes.

Perhaps this traditional element gives us something to go on, even though the picture derived from the four reports is not complete or free from ambiguity. One thinks of the work of Milman Parry and Albert B. Lord on traditional oral narrative poetry and the two elements identified as "formula" and "theme" which bulk large in their discussion (Lord, 1960). The second of these, the theme, was described in the earlier writings of Lord as a compositional device, a large building block, used by oral poets in producing narrative poetry. A frequently quoted definition gives the theme as a "recurrent element of narration or description in traditional oral poetry" (Lord, 1951:73).

But before pursuing this any further, another matter must be touched on: the question of genre in folk narrative. There is no need to become embroiled in a sticky debate over terminology, since definitions are not critical for what follows. The kind of stories examined in the field studies with their cast of stock fictional characters and their stock of remarkable incidents and events were mostly what one might call folktales. These stories are certainly different from the kind of historical legend found in the Bible. Does this, then, mean that any connection between the kind of folktale transmission noted in the field studies and any presumed oral transmission of biblical legends is unlikely?

Two of the authors of the field studies discussed above did mention the existence of stories like legends among the material they encountered in their research. Consciously avoiding standard terminology for Limba stories, Finnegan refers to this kind of story as historical narrative (Finnegan, 1967:140). She points out that these stories are both like and unlike the kinds of folktales which were the main object of study in her book. Occasional stories about the great figures of the past were similar in many ways to the folktales. But the more or less official stories transmitted in the families of chiefs were much less like the folktales. This difference was largely due to the fact that they had a rather serious function pertaining to the maintenance of the status of chiefly families. In her more general work on African oral literature, Finnegan does give a working definition for legend (Finnegan, 1970:367ff.) but perhaps her most important comment in this regard is the closing sentence of her brief discussion of this topic.

> Altogether much more research needs to be done on the indigenous contexts, tone, and classifications of 'historical narratives' before we can make assertions about them (Finnegan, 1970:373).

Similarly, Dégh concentrates in her study on what she calls either "folktale" or "*märchen*" as the most important type in her investigation. Even so, other types were encountered and received brief treatment, especially some varieties of the legend. She points out that there are significant differences between the folktale and the legend, here referring to a continuing discussion of this general subject especially among European folklorists (Lüthi, 1967; Röhrich, 1965). In an earlier article, Dégh has provided fuller discussions of legends than is found in her book (Dégh, 1965b). In this article, she sums up the nature of the legend this way:

> The legend's essential characteristics are looseness of form and content, oscillating around a stable nucleus, and its attachment to real life and belief. (78)

It appears, however, that in both the book and the article the main kind of legend used as a basis for discussion is the belief legend which has to do with experiences of the supernatural, like dealings with witches. Still, one of the narrators among the people of Kakasd studied by Dégh was a man who could tell legends of a historical type as well as *märchen*. Incidentally, he loved books and was well read (Dégh, 1969:235ff.). Even with this narrator a difference can be seen between telling legends and telling *märchen*.

As a teller of legends he exhibited a different attitude from that of the storyteller; his texts tried to be realistic and he treated them differently than a *märchen*. (Dégh, 1969:237)

Unfortunately for our purposes, Dégh did not pursue the transmission of the legend of the historical type and its relationship to the folktale.

Both Finnegan and Dégh alert us to the fact that there are important differences between the folktale and the legend. But neither has provided an analysis of the legend as a part of their field studies. Are we then left without any basis whatsoever for assuming a sufficient continuity between folktales and some kinds of legends to expect some legends to be transmitted like the folktales described above in the field studies? More specifically, are some legends also transmitted with flexibility so that traditional elements like stock episodes become important devices in building narratives? There are some clues and suggestions to go on. Dégh and others have made the general observation that the same motifs are widely shared by *märchen*, myth, and legend (Dégh, 1969:60; Hain, 1971:256).

If, as we have seen, Dégh includes under the term "motif" those traditional elements of different kinds which are used in building folktales, then it would seem that these elements can appear and function in a similar way in legend. Some support for this comes from some general comments about Hungarian folklore in the introduction to her collection of Hungarian folk narratives already mentioned. When speaking of the multiplicity of episodes and the way in which a framework holds together a string of episodes chosen by the narrator, Dégh remarks that this phenomenon is most notable in the *märchen* but "more or less characteristic also of the other genres" (Dégh, 1965a:xxx). She adds, however, that the Hungarian historical legends are "the most roughly structured" so that "usually they tell of a single episode with no effort at epic elaboration" (xxxvii). Thus, the possibility is at least open that the kind of transmission described above for folktales may apply for legends as well.

ORAL PROSE AND ORAL POETRY

It was suggested above that there was some similarity between the picture gained from the field studies and the description of compositional devices in the work of Parry and Lord on oral narrative poetry. As a matter of fact, Lord has produced a small study of oral prose (Lord, 1962). While this is not a field study, it is worth pursuing in some detail because it sets the discussion of oral prose in the context of the study of oral literature as a whole. Lord's work is an introductory article to a collection of Angolan tales in which he offers comments on the tales from the point of view of his work in collecting and analyzing oral poetry. Lord's attitude can be seen from the following quotation:

> Repetition of incidents and repeated patterns of incidents are, moreover, characteristic compositional devices of oral style. The story teller, in prose as well as in verse, needs a repertory not only of common phrases but also of frequently recurring incidents and groups of incidents in order to rebuild any tale in its retelling or even to remember it as he listens to it for the first time. Such common incidents and patterns are a mark of oral literature. (xiii)

In Lord's view, the striking point of similarity between the work on oral narrative poetry and the tales from Angola is the repeated use of larger blocks of material, incidents and patterns of incidents, which Lord calls "themes." Themes are defined in this article as "repeated incidents and descriptions" which are "the narrative building blocks of any story tradition" (xvi). With themes the repetition is rarely exact. The wording usually varies. The repetition here is repetition of elements of content like scenes, incidents, and descriptions, which recur with variable wording (Culley, 1967:18). Clusters or groupings of themes which recur Lord calls "patterns."

In speaking about repetition in the Angolan stories, Lord first mentions internal repetition, or repetition of similar incidents within the same story. In some cases, there is progression in which several different characters in turn take the leading role in a repeated incident. The cumulative tale is another example of internal repetition. Lord calls these various kinds of internal repetitions "the theme of repetition itself," meaning apparently that the structure of repetition itself functions as a compositional device in constructing tales (xvi).

But repetition also occurs when incidents appear in more than one tale. As an example of this, Lord mentions what he calls the theme of distraction:

> The theme of distraction is found especially, it would seem, in those tales in which a series of people (or more frequently and perhaps, significantly, animals) attempt to do something but are distracted therefrom; only the hero steps in finally and does not yield to distraction.(xix)

Lord is prepared to include among the examples of the distraction theme not only instances where the attention is drawn by something of interest but also instances where the attention is drawn by something frightening. After examining a few examples of distractions, some frightening and some pleasant, Lord goes on to say that these examples are "multiforms of a single idea, either 'thunder,' or 'dance,' as distractions" (xx). This statement is intriguing since it suggests that defining the theme may be more complicated than is implied by the usual definition given by Lord, namely, repeated incidents and descriptions. There are actually two different kinds of similarities being introduced here by Lord without being clearly identified. On the one hand, a grouping can be made on the basis of similarity in content. All stories are grouped together in which a sound like thunder frightens everyone off except the hero. Then again, all stories may be grouped together in which an activity like a dance attracts everyone but the hero. This would lead to two groups: thunder as a distraction and dance as a distraction. On the other hand, a grouping can be made on the basis of similarity of function. The thunder and the dance do the same thing. They both provide distraction.

In fact, Lord appears to be aware of the distinction just mentioned when he introduces another group of examples and points out that there exist "some stories, or parts of stories, that, in spite of difference of subject matter, are clearly the same as far as framework or structure is concerned" (xx). Here Lord is referring specifically to two narratives in which some sort of barrier is set up which allows the innocent through but not the guilty. One of these involves a bridge. The other has to do with a mountain. Lord argues that "by placing the two side by side we can see one of the useful frames in the composition of these tales" (xxi). Here, the similarity rests on the function rather than the content. While aware of the distinction between similarity in content and similarity in function, Lord does not reflect this awareness in his definition of theme nor does he discuss the possible implications.

Lord also distinguishes groups or clusters of themes which often amount to story patterns or plots. As Lord is well aware, some of these plots can be found in the tale traditions of many different peoples. Here, too, a complicating factor emerges. While it may be urged that oral narrators use patterns as a device for story building, the apparent universality of story patterns is by no means completely explained by this. The same plots seem to arise spontaneously at different times and in different places.

Lord's description of themes and patterns can be pursued further by consulting his work on oral narrative poetry, especially *The Singer of Tales* (Lord, 1960), in which these devices were defined, described, and fully illustrated. Here, Lord makes the suggestion that the presence of themes in narrative may not be due completely to the needs of the singer. He speaks of a "deeper significance, perhaps deriving from ritual" (89). Especially when talking about story patterns, clusters of themes which make up a story, Lord employs the word "myth," often describing story patterns in terms of myths about dying and rising gods (175, 186). At the end of his book, Lord makes this comment.

> The traditional oral epic singer is not an artist; he is a seer. The patterns of thought that he has inherited came into being to serve not *art* but religion in its most basic sense. (220)

There is no need to pursue any further this idea of a myth and ritual background for themes and patterns or to examine its validity. It is enough to see that in discussing these subjects Lord goes beyond the simple matter of devices in oral composition.

In a recent article on oral narrative poetry, Lord says that he would be willing to accept a clarification in the general area of theme (1973). Two new terms are introduced: "compositional themes" and "type-scenes." Compositional themes are described as repeated elements of narrative which have a considerable degree of similarity of wording. This similarity of wording is taken to indicate very clearly that the singer is using these elements of narrative, the compositional themes, as a device of oral composition. The singer is employing ready-made units of narrative which nevertheless can be applied to different parts of the same narrative or used in different narratives. Even with a significant degree of similarity in wording, these compositional themes have flexibility. The type-scenes, on the other hand, "contain a given set of repeated elements or details, not all of which are always present, nor always in the same order, but enough of which are present to make the scene a recognizable one" (207). Such type-scenes are also characteristic of oral epic according to Lord.

When Lord's comments are set beside the four field studies, it looks as though the elements variously referred to as "stock incident," "episode," and "core-plot" may be closely related to the elements Lord identified as theme in prose and as compositional theme, type-scene, and story pattern in poetry. If this is so, then the base for discussion can be broadened to bring in some aspects of the discussion of themes and the like from oral poetry in order to fill out the discussion of similar items found in oral prose.

While this broadening of the discussion will likely prove helpful, Lord's discussion has raised a number of problems of definition and description which indicate that the discussion of theme in oral narrative poetry is by no means finished. Among the matters which will need some attention in the future is the question of how many different elements we are really dealing with in this general area of theme. We are dealing with different kinds of repeated patterns. How many must be distinguished in terms of their nature and function? As we have seen, Lord's discussion shows an awareness of certain basic distinctions which have to be made. Lord speaks of a compositional theme the nature and function of which centers on high verbal similarity. This verbal similarity makes them easily identifiable elements in oral narrative poetry. Type-scenes are repeated patterns of elements with little or no verbal similarity. These, then, would appear to be identified on the basis of similar content rather than similar wording. Although, as we have seen in Lord's treatment of Angolan tales, he allows for identification of themes through similarity in function — that is, when similar things happen even though they are presented in terms of different subject matter. These cannot be identified by similarity in content but only on the basis of a similar story function. Then, too, Lord speaks of a story pattern which seems to be the grouping of themes which make up a story. Lord can speak rather more generally in this area, as for example when he refers to the long Homeric poems by remarking that the "essential pattern of the *Iliad* is the same as that of the *Odyssey*: they are both the story of an absence that causes havoc to the beloved of the absentee and of his return to set matters aright" (Lord, 1960:186). Here we are talking about a pattern which is less specific and more abstract than those mentioned so far, since the two Homeric poems do not have the same content and tell different stories. Furthermore, in terms of how these patterns function for the singer, Lord speaks of mythic patterns rather than compositional devices. Finally, it may be noted that Lord has introduced a further refinement with the use of the word "motif" when referring to another kind of pattern. In mentioning the work of some scholars of Old and Middle English, Lord would prefer "to designated as motifs what they call themes and to reserve the term theme for a structural unit that has semantic essence but can never be divorced from its form, even if its form be constantly variable and multiform" (Lord, 1960:198). The scholarly discussion of oral narrative poetry has brought out one further point that needs to be mentioned. The division between poetry composed in an oral formulaic tradition where formulas and themes are major devices and poetry composed in writing by literate poets is not dramatic in the sense that there is total discontinuity. Especially in the case of Anglo-Saxon poetry, scholars have found the presence of repeated, traditional phrases and stock scenes in poems which were apparently composed in writing. Lord is now prepared to apply the terms "transitional" or "mixed" to such poems to indicate the marked relationship they bear to oral traditional poetry (Lord, 1973:200-10). It is enough to mention this scholarly discussion about oral composition and literary composition in oral narrative poetry. One may expect that any consideration of orally composed prose as compared to written prose will similarly lead into complex and difficult areas.

ORAL PROSE AND BIBLICAL STUDIES

While it is by no means uncommon in the writings of biblical scholars to find references to the oral stage of prose traditions, there has been no concerted, systematic attempt to relate contemporary discussions about oral prose to the biblical material. However, some work in the New Testament field can be mentioned. Thorlief Boman has used the work of a number of European folklorists in his sketch of the nature of oral tradition which he then applies to the Jesus tradition (Boman, 1967). Although Boman has gathered a great deal of useful information, one of his conclusions appears curious in the light of the field studies referred to above. He remarks that an established result of recent folklore study is that "die Volkserzähler zu allen Zeiten und in allen Ländern ein so gutes Gedächtnis haben, dass sie imstande sind, eine grosse Zahl langer Geschichten ihr ganzes Leben hindurch wortgetreu im Gedächtnis zu behalten und wiederzugeben" (11). That fixed transmission is possible has not been disputed above. It appears to be an option which must be taken seriously. Still, examples of fixed transmission cannot be used as a model of how all prose is transmitted orally. In fact, the field studies discussed earlier, which were deliberately selected because they represented examples of careful analysis based on close observation, suggest that the unfixed form of transmission is quite common and may well be far more characteristic of oral tradition than the fixed form.

Also in the New Testament field, Erhardt Güttgemanns has devoted a section of his book on the form criticism of the Gospels to the problem of oral versus written as seen in the context of some recent literary and linguistic studies (Güttgemanns, 1971). He refers to Lord's book, *Singer of Tales*, but his main interest lies in the relevance of Lord's work for the description of what happened, to Gospel tradition in the transition from oral to written. Güttgemanns seems to be mainly interested in arguing that the kind of distinction drawn by Lord between oral and written literature renders doubtful any hypothesis maintaining a smooth transition from an oral period to a period of writing in Gospel tradition (148ff.; also Klemm, 1972). However, it was suggested above that the discussion of this difficult matter is still going on (Lord, 1973; for a different application of Lord's work, see Güttgemanns, 1973:3).

In the field of Old Testament studies, the work of three scholars may be referred to briefly. The first is Dorothy Irving Thompson. In a study of messenger stories in Genesis (1970), she describes a new literary unit which she claims is characteristic of Near Eastern narrative. This she calls "the pattern." Working from a very early study of Milman Parry on the traditional epithet, Thompson speculates that patterns function for the narrator of oral prose in the way that epithets or standard phrases do for narrators of oral poetry. Since her work does not seem to take into account the later discussions of theme by Parry and Lord, what Thompson means by pattern seems to be a more abstract outline than that usually associated with theme, at least the compositional theme which requires a significant degree of verbal similarity. Thompson's pattern is perhaps closer to the type-scene. Thus, Thompson's study raises the question of patterns in narrative which may be due to the demands of producing narrative in oral performance.

The second scholar is David M. Gunn. In an article, "Narrative Patterns and Oral Tradition in Judges and Samuel" (1974a), Gunn presents a careful attempt to isolate conventional and stereotyped patterns in biblical narrative which may well "reflect traditional composition but also quite possibly *oral* traditional composition" (286). Gunn begins with the Hebrew text first in order to establish a case for the existence of patterns which appear to be stereotyped and traditional. Then, he attempts to show that a likely source for many of these traditional patterns may be a tradition of oral narration. For a description of what happens in the transmission of oral prose, Gunn has relied on more general statements of folklorists to the effect that typical descriptions and episodes are very much a part of oral prose style. Gunn relates these typical elements to the themes of Parry and Lord so that he may then expand his discussion of stereotyped, traditional patterns in the light of the work done on oral poetry, especially by Lord. Thus, Gunn's references to the work of folklorists on oral prose is rather limited (although more references are found in Gunn, 1974b). Nor is the problem of the definition of theme taken up in any detail. Nevertheless, Gunn's discussion of the Hebrew evidence is valuable and raises a number of points which will have to be taken up in subsequent discussions of patterns in narrative. For one thing, the patterns isolated by Gunn are relatively short, being segments of narrative which are parts of a larger story. Similarity in wording is an important clue for identification, as is true for Lord's compositional themes. In a second article on the same general subject (1974b), Gunn endeavors to reply to some proposals by John Van Seters, who is the third scholar whose work must be considered.

In *Abraham in History and Tradition*, John Van Seters has offered a very full study of the Abraham stories and presented a wide-ranging critique of many aspects of the scholarly discussion of this material. Oral tradition is one topic about which Van Seters has made a number of comments, and so it is necessary to make a brief assessment of his views on this subject.

Van Seters points to the problem which has also emerged in the preceding pages — the general lack of a thorough study of oral tradition with regard to prose. He is, however, concerned with two areas: oral tradition and scribal tradition (158ff.). Both in his general discussion of theory as well as in his specific analysis of texts, Van Seters seeks to mark out the differences between oral and written composition, at least insofar as the Abraham traditions are concerned. In general terms, he is fairly confident that one can identify the parts of the Abraham tradition that have come from oral tradition or bear the marks of oral style and the parts that are the result of literary composition. The main device used by Van Seters to distinguish between oral style and scribal or literary style is the set of "epic laws" proposed by Axel Olrik in his famous article, "Epic Laws of Folk Narrative" (English translation, 1965). These laws are thirteen headings which sum up what Olrik believes to be the rules or constraints which regulate folk narrative. Van Seters lists ten of these in his book (160f.). When it comes to the nature of scribal tradition, he is less specific, pointing out that examples of scribal tradition are available, such as the Assyrian and Babylonian royal inscriptions, the Synoptic gospels, early Arabic literature, and the Icelandic sagas (162). More specifically, Van Seters' discussion is directed toward the subject of variants and the extent to which oral variants can be distinguished from written, since his approach to the Abraham stories starts with a consideration of the famous doublets. In preparation for this, he sets down a few points of comparison which, he argues, reflect important differences between oral and written compositional variants.

Van Seters has gone into considerable detail, and this will merit fuller discussion in the future. However, it will have to suffice here to indicate briefly the main problem I experience with his proposals. To put it succinctly, I feel that it is premature to suggest that we can define the nature and characteristics of oral and scribal tradition with sufficient clarity to be able to identify with a great deal of confidence those segments of the Abraham stories which lie close to oral tradition and those which are the result of literary composition.

One of the main problems is how to evaluate the work of Olrik. It is not clear that Olrik provides a sound basis for a series of criteria which can be used in a very close analysis of texts in order to determine material akin to oral and material stemming from written composition. Even though the famous article by Olrik has for long been highly regarded in many quarters, including biblical studies, the work of Olrik was deliberately excluded from the discussion of the nature of oral prose composition earlier in this part. In the first place, Olrik's article was not a specific description of field work as were the four studies by Crowley, Finnegan, Dégh, and Scheub, nor did Olrik intend it to be. He chose to focus on broad characteristics which his years of experience with folk literature suggested to him. He began by positing a broad category which he called "*Sage*" and which included myth, song, heroic saga, and local legend. Thus, his laws or principles are restricted to the kind of general observations which will apply to a number of different genres, both prose and poetry. In the light of the nature of Olrik's study, one may well ask to what extent his set of laws can provide a test which can be applied to specific texts in order to determine with a fair degree of certainty whether a text stems from oral or written composition. It would appear that this would have to be tested carefully in a controlled situation. It is also likely that his laws would have to be stated more precisely if they were going to be used for purposes of testing. This is not so much to question Olrik's impressions of what frequently happens in a broad range of oral narrative prose and poetry as to question whether or not they represent a fine enough instrument to be used in making decisions about specific texts like the Abraham narratives. Even so, questions about the validity of his observations have been raised. It has been argued by William O. Hendricks that Olrik's laws can be applied successfully to written literature. Hendricks has attempted to show that "the structural principles which underlie the composition of folklore narratives are similar — if not identical — to those that underlie literary narratives" (1970:86). If Hendricks were correct, or even partly correct, the use of Olrik's laws to distinguish oral from written would be called into question rather seriously. At the very least, more investigation and discussion is needed.

If the situation is less than clear on the oral tradition side, there is also need for further clarification on the literary or, more precisely, the scribal tradition side. It has already been mentioned above that Van Seters referred to some areas (royal inscriptions, the Synoptic Gospels, Arabic and Icelandic literature) which he thought might provide some excellent examples of a writer borrowing written compositions to which he has access and incorporating them into his work. It is unfortunate that Van Seters did not have time to expand his discussion of these materials because it would have been very helpful and, indeed, is necessary before a clear case can be established for "guidelines on the relationships of variants to literary dependence"(162f.).

There is a further problem which will be picked up in the discussion of the biblical texts in Part II. Are we reduced to two simple options here, one oral and the other literary, and both clearly distinguishable from each other?

Thus, Van Seters's views should probably be taken as suggestive rather than definitive. If taken as an indication of problems to be solved and areas to be clarified, his comments are extremely useful. His work has demanded, in effect, that we take the description not only of oral tradition but also scribal tradition seriously. Such a demand is fully justified.

CONCLUDING COMMENTS

The four field studies reaffirmed what many folklorists have observed for a long time: oral transmisnion of stories is often a very flexible process in which narrators recompose traditional stories during performance. But to say that the oral transmission of prose is frequently unfixed does not mean that the process is simply free improvisation. There appear to be both stability and flexibility in creation and transmission. The stability resides to a large part in the traditional elements which are so much a part of the process of story-telling. In the field studies, it was seen that something described variously as stock scene, incident, episode, or core-plot was identified as a building block for the construction of narrative. Such traditional elements appear to be very flexible in that they can be expanded, adapted, elaborated, and linked together in many different ways. Much more discussion, analysis, and description is required to ascertain the extent to which we may speak of a common device of oral prose composition. Still, the fact that such building blocks, frequently called themes, have been identified and examined in some detail in oral narrative poetry lends support to the idea of a similar compositional device in prose narrative.

However, the assumption of the use of traditional building blocks as an important mark and characteristic of orally composed prose narratives does not yet provide a handy test which can quickly separate orally composed narratives from narratives composed in writing but is best seen as an interesting clue to be followed. The lack of a broadly applicable definition and description of such a device in oral prose has already been mentioned. While the study of a device like this is further advanced for oral narrative poetry, it must be said that the scholarly discussion in this regard is still very much "in progress." It appears that different kinds of patterns can be detected (motif, compositional theme, type scene, story pattern) and that additional clarification is needed to establish more accurately what these patterns are. Some of these seem to be characteristic of oral poetry because they are compositional devices, although such traditional patterns may continue to appear in written poetry. Others seem to appear in both oral and written narrative and thus may be patterns fundamental to all narrative.

In a sense, this discussion of oral narrative prose extends an invitation to explore different kinds of repeated patterns at different levels of the text. Consequently, Part II will pick up the question of oral composition of prose by looking at some repeated patterns in biblical material, some stories, episodes, and scenes which appear more than once. This will also contribute to the discussion already going on among biblical scholars (Gunn, Van Seters) about oral and written prose. At the same time, the comparison of biblical material will permit a resumption of the discussion already initiated in Part I about the nature of variants and about similarities and differences found in texts. This will also prepare for the investigation to be carried out in Part III.

In Part III, the focus will be shifted to a different aspect of pattern or structure. In looking for stock scenes and episodes, the emphasis is on a large or significant amount of identical material, a very high level of similarity in content. At the same time, it was seen that different elements of content could have the same function. Different characters could play the same role. Different actions do the same thing in the plot. Comparing stories from this point of view leads to the exploration of more generalized or abstracted narrative frameworks which lie behind stories which on the surface may not at first glance be very similar or have many details of content in common. While investigation of this sort may still be relevant to oral composition and transmission, it is probably more relevant to the investigation of the structure of literature as such. Thus, in Part III, some samplings of biblical material will be examined from the point of view of similarity in underlying story frameworks.

Part II

Oral Transmission and Biblical Texts

The aim of this part will be to examine some of the examples of parallel accounts in the Hebrew narrative tradition of the Bible in the light of the preceding discussion of oral prose transmission, and particularly the stock scene or episode as a device of narrative construction used by oral narrators. The parallels to be used are well known, and fairly few in number. It is true that the lack of any sizeable body of evidence to work with does not invite optimism with regard to developing any serious conclusions, especially since, as has been seen, the discussion of oral prose transmission provides interesting clues rather than a handy test for the oral nature of material. Still, it is appropriate to make a rapid survey of most of the parallel material, particularly since it does not seem that the parallels have been studied as a group. At least, I have not run into any study of this sort. In addition, this survey will permit further discussion of the nature of similarities and differences in terms of content, function, and structure, and this time with biblical material. This will prepare the way for the kind of analysis to be explored in Part III.

A. *A Patriarch, his Wife, and a Foreign Ruler*
   (Genesis 12:10-20, Genesis 20, and Genesis 26:1-13 or 14)

These three stories are perhaps the most famous example of a group of biblical narratives which bear a marked resemblance to each other. For purposes of comparison, the main features of these three stories may be summarized in the following chart.

Genesis 12:10-20	Genesis 20	Genesis 26:1-13 or 14
Abram and Sarai.	Abraham and Sarah.	Isaac and Rebecca.
Famine.		Famine.

33

Egypt.	Gerar.	Gerar.
		Yahweh Speech
Fear of life because of wife. Proposed deception.	Deception. (No reason given)	Deception. Fear of life because of wife.
Wife taken by Pharaoh because of beauty.	Wife taken by Abimelech. (No reason given)	Wife not taken.
Yahweh intervened with punishment.	Elohim intervened in a dream: "give wife back."	Abimelech accidentally discovered truth.
Pharaoh *called to* Abram *and said:* "*What* then *have you done* to me?	Abimelech *called to* Abraham *and said:* "*What have you done* to us?	Amibelech *called to* Isaac *and said:. . . .* Abimelech said: "*What then have you done* to us?
	Abraham gave reason for his deception: fear of life because of wife.	
Abram sent off with escort.	Abimelech gave presents and wife.	Abimelech gave protection. Isaac did well.
	Abraham prayed and Elohim healed.	

Similarities can be reviewed very readily by looking at the characters, setting, and actions. The characters are not the same in all three stories. Abraham (Abram) and Sarah (Sarai) feature in two stories. Isaac and Rebecca appear in the other. The ruler is Pharaoh in one story but Abimilech in the other two. Yet, even though the names of the persons change, the roles remain much the same. The hero is a partriarch who enters foreign territory with his beautiful wife. The person taken in by the deception is a foreign ruler. The setting varies also, being Egypt or Gerar depending on the ruler involved. But the locale is still a foreign territory. The main actions or events common to the three stories are in most instances alike. The patriarch enters a foreign land. The patriarch employs a deception which is essentially the same in each case: he lets on that his wife is his sister. After the discovery of the truth, the foreign ruler summons the patriarch and reproaches him for his action. Nevertheless, one action crucial to the plot takes a different form in one of the stories. In Genesis 12 and 20, the foreign ruler becomes aware of the patriarch's deception because of divine intervention, although even this takes two forms, punishment in the first story and a dream in the second. In contrast, the foreign ruler of Genesis 26 becomes aware of the deception accidentally when he sees something he was not supposed to see, namely Isaac having a rendezvous with Rebecca. Yet, while this action is of a different order in this last story, the function of this element is the same in all three: the deception is revealed and the truth comes out.

It is worth noticing that similarity has been viewed in two ways in the preceding paragraph. There was identity in content where the names of persons and places are the same and where the actions performed are virtually the same. But there were also instances in which the roles remained the same, although filled by characters with different names. Similarly, there was one instance of actions functioning the same way in the story even though the actions are different. However, the next step is to investigate how the correspondences are patterned within each of the three stories.

The story about Abram and Sarai in Genesis 12 is remarkably concise. Famine is given as the reason for the move into foreign territory. The deception is presented in the form of a proposal made by Abram to Sarai that she pose as his sister. This was necessary, according to Abram, because her beauty would put his life in danger. Normally, a proposal like this would have been followed by a description of how this was carried out. This brief narrative omits this step, allowing the statement of the proposal itself to suggest that the matter mentioned was done. On entry into Egypt, Abram's fears prove true. His wife is taken by Pharaoh because of her great beauty. But because of the deception Abram does well. Up to this point, the story forms a kind of episode in itself: danger/deception/danger averted. But the story does not stop here because the solution is not entirely satisfactory. Abram has remained alive and prospered, but Pharaoh's harem is no fit place to leave a patriarch's wife, quite apart from the astonishing fact that she got there at all. In other words, the solution to the first problem, the danger to Abram's life, contains within itself another problem demanding a solution. At this point Yahweh intervenes and strikes Pharaoh with various afflictions. This is understood by the narrator as punishment for taking Sarai. Curiously enough, there is no explanation of how Pharaoh learned the reason for his troubles but the narrative moves immediately to his summoning of Abram, reproaching him in a series of rhetorical questions, and his sending him off with Sarai. Thus, this last part forms a kind of episode in itself as well: problem/divine intervention/problem solved.

One might outline the action of the story of Genesis 12 in the following way.

(a) On entering a foreign country, a partriarch fears he will be in danger of his life because of his beautiful wife. (Problem)
(b) The patriarch pretends that his wife is his sister. (Deception)
(c) The patriarch's wife is taken by the foreign ruler but the patriarch remains alive and well. (Problem solved) This situation is not normal and cannot continue. (New problem)
(d) The divinity intervenes with punishment so that the truth is revealed. (Divine intervention)
(e) The foreign ruler summons the Patriarch, reproaches him for his deception and gives him back his wife. (Problem solved)

The second account, Genesis 20, runs differently at a number of points. No explanation, such as famine, is offered for the entry into foreign territory. Then too, Abraham tells an apparent lie, yet no reason is given for this until the end of the narrative. Perhaps the narrator responsible for the present form of the story assumed that the reader or listener would be aware of the wife-sister ploy and the reason for it. Similarly, the bare statement that Abimelech took Sarah is left without further explanation. Thus, the deception along with the explanation for it and the taking of the wife both of which appeared to be significant steps in the narrative of Genesis 12 seem here to be reduced to background information leading up to the intervention of Elohim in a dream to Abimelech. In the dream itself, an interesting pattern is followed. Abimelech's crime is revealed and a punishment is announced. Abimelech makes an appeal. Yahweh accepts it and gives instructions as to how the situation can be restored to normal. Here, the divine intervention with the foreign ruler, handled so briefly in Genesis 12, has been elaborated considerably. The summoning of the patriarch and the reproach follow. It is at this point, in Abraham's reply to Abimelech, that all the explanations come which might have been expected earlier in the narrative. Abraham tells why he claimed Sarah was his sister, adding that this was not a lie because she really was his sister. Abraham and Sarah then receive valuable gifts from Abimelech. It is added that Abraham prayed to Elohim who healed a condition which had apparently been afflicting Abimelech's household and which was a punishment for taking Sarah. This last matter is curious because it was not mentioned earlier in the story, except conceivably in the instruction of Yahweh earlier where it was said that Abraham would pray for Abimelech if Sarah were returned.

Since the aim here is not to pursue all the problems and potential difficulties presented by a given story, a number of interesting matters are being passed over in favor of restricting discussion to a broad comparison. Looking at Genesis 12 and 20 from the point of view of how the individual elements are patterned or arranged, the two versions are rather different, even though they have many elements in common. It was suggested that Genesis 12 had two episodes with a problem / problem-solved structure in which the first problem was solved by the cleverness and resourcefulness of the hero and the second was solved by divine intervention. But the outline given above for Genesis 12 could not be used for Genesis 20. Here, the matter of deception appears to be little more than background information with the result that the story seems to focus on the one episode consisting of the taking of the woman, the divine intervention, and her restoration to her husband. Then too, paralleling the demonstration of the invulnerability of the patriarch under divine protection even in foreign territory, there is the concern for the innocent foreign ruler. The foreign king is not the wicked despot who gets what he deserves but the well meaning ruler who is innocent of an intentional wrong and who seeks to do the honorable thing once he knows the truth.

Like Genesis 12, the story of Genesis 26 uses famine as the reason for the move into foreign territory. A speech of Yahweh at the beginning tells Isaac not to go to Egypt, a comment which seems to show an awareness of the Abram story of Genesis 12. This, added to the promises which follow about the land and the descendants, suggests that the speech is written from the point of view of a framework much larger than the narrative itself and so performs the function of linking the narrative to a larger block of material. However this may be, the speech does not seem to play a vital role in the narrative of Genesis 26:1-13 or 14, since it is not referred to again and, if left out, would not be missed as far as the development of the story is concerned.

In Genesis 26 the deception element is developed in a similar way to the Genesis 12 story. Isaac tells people that his wife is his sister. The reason given is that he fears for his life because of his wife's beauty. However, the story of Genesis 26 differs from the other two in that the patriarch's wife is not taken by the foreign ruler. Even so, the deception is discovered, although by a simple accident rather than divine intervention. This leads to the summoning of the patriarch and the reproach by the foreign king. In this case, the reproach is expressed in terms of what might have happened as a result of this deception, the possibility of a crime followed by inevitable punishment, rather than crime already committed and punishment being suffered. Isaac ends up in a favorable situation with the ruler's protection.

This story is curious for a number of reasons. The patriarch fears for his life and performs a deception but his wife was not taken. The comments of the king later on suggest that the danger was more imagined than real. If this is so, then the patriarch does not emerge as someone who is clever and resourceful. He performs an unnecessary deception and even gets caught at it. In any case, the problem/problem-solved tension which was very strong in Genesis 12, being repeated in two episodes there, is considerably weaker in this story due to the apparent lack of any real danger. One can still, perhaps, discern two story movements in a shadowy way. The patriarch thinks he faces danger, a first problem. He performs a deception but what he fears does not come true. A second problem can be seen in the fact that the deception exists, maintaining an abnormal situation. When the truth is revealed to the foreign ruler, he restores the situation to normal, bestowing his protection, so that all ends well. However, the shape of the story suggests rather the hero as a bumbler who in spite of his inept handling of the situation comes out on top. Possibly, the unnecessary deception set beside the absurdity of the discovery is central. However this may be, the outline for Genesis 12 set down above could not serve as an outline for this story.

This brief review of the three stories has shown that they are both similar and different in important ways. Considering the ways in which the narratives are similar, one finds it difficult to avoid the conclusion that they are versions of the same story or, to put it another way, the similarities cannot be due to coincidence. At the same time, each version is different in the selection of elements and the emphasis given to the elements, and this is why it was not helpful to draw up a common outline of action of the three stories. It was argued above that the outline set out for Genesis 12 does not prove adequate to reflect the key movements and tensions of Genesis 20 and 26.

This group of three stories has received considerable attention over the years in commentaries, in special studies (recently, for example, Koch, Petersen, Schmitt), and in passing comments. These stories are also treated in some detail in Van Seters's book (1975). The relationship of these stories to each other has been explained in many ways. There is no clear cut answer, and making any decision is a delicate matter. There seem to be two general positions evident in scholarly discussion. One sees the three stories as oral variants. The other seeks to explain the existence of three versions in terms of a literary process of redaction.

Since it has long been known that versions of stories multiply in oral tradition, it is quite in order to entertain the possibility that the three stories found in Genesis 12, 20, and 26 are three versions which developed in oral tradition (for example, Koch). However, those holding this view frequently move on to an attempt to establish which story must have been the earliest and which the latest. In view of the field studies considered above, identifying earlier and later versions of the "same" story would seem to be much more hazardous than generally imagined. In the kind of transmission studied above, there is no "original" version. There exists a remarkable flexibility. The shape of a given version depends on a number of things: the occasion of the performance, the narrator's personality, and the narrator's creative ability. Variables like these make it extremely difficult to present a convincing case for a chronological development of the three Genesis stories. Still, even if the question of chronology is murky, it can be said that the three stories do reflect a stability and change which may well be the result of oral transmission. The group of common elements set out above provide the raw material of the three narratives, each of which has assumed its own shape and has something different to say. The variations can be explained in terms of expansion, reduction, restatement, and rearrangement of these common elements. If one were to argue that we have here three versions of a stock episode, then the stock episode would have to be defined in terms of the common elements. But one cannot argue that this is so, only that it may be so. The stability and flexibility reflected in the three versions appear to be compatible with the description of oral transmission given in the field studies.

The second explanation turns to a literary rather than an oral process. Some time ago, Samuel Sandmel traced the presence of different versions of a story, especially the three Genesis stories being discussed here, to a redactional activity he called "haggadic" (1961:121; for a critique, Childs, 1972:48-50). According to this theory, the writer retells a story in order to emend it, "neutralizing by addition" (120). This view has received some support from F. V. Winnett (1965:6) and Norman E. Wagner (1967:230-231). Having stated his preference for a literary explanation in an earlier article (1972:197), Van Seters has presented a detailed argument for his views in the book already discussed above, *Abraham in History and Tradition* (1975). According to Van Seters, the first story (Genesis 12) is the oldest and still in its "primitive folktale form" (183). The second story (Genesis 20) is a "literary compositional variant" of the first. The third story (Genesis 26) is "a literary conflation of both the other stories" due to the fact that the author is deliberately making Isaac's life parallel to Abraham's at this point. It was argued above that Van Seters has proposed an option which has to be taken seriously. Still, it was also argued that a lack of clarity about oral tradition was matched by a lack of clarity about scribal tradition. If distinguishing oral from written variants is not as easy as Van Seters suggests, then the problem of why there are three versions of the so-called wife-sister story is still open for discussion. It appears possible to develop plausible arguments on both sides: the three versions are a result of oral tradition or literary tradition. At this point, one may ask whether we are faced with two simple choices or are there intermediate possibilities which need to be defined? We will have to come back to this question when all the examples have been reviewed.

B. *At the Well*
(Genesis 24:10-14, Genesis 29:1-14, and Exodus 2:15-21)

These sections portray a meeting at a well which leads at a later point, although not within these sections, to a marriage. In order to show the similarities, the accounts may be summarized in the following chart.

Genesis 24:10-33	*Genesis 29:1-14*	*Exodus 2:15-21*
Servant sent by Abraham in Isaac's interest to Aram Naharaim.	Jacob, (a fugitive?) went to land of Easterners.	Moses, a fugitive went to land of Midian
Stopped at a well.	Stopped at a well.	Stopped at a well.
Proposed sign.	Discussion with shepherds. (learned with relatives)	
Girl came to draw water. Watered camels (i.e. sign happened).	Rachel identified as his relative came to water sheep.	Seven daughters of priest came to water flocks.
Gave her gift. Asked her name and learned with relations of master. Asked if can stay.	Rolled away stone and watered flocks.	Saved them from shepherds and watered flocks.
Girl ran home and told.	Girl ran home and told.	Girls went to father and told.
Brother, Laban, came to servant. Invited him home.	Father, Laban, came and brought him home.	Father gave orders to invite him.
(Marriage occurred).	(Marriage occurred).	(Marriage occurred).

This outline presents a synoptic view of the similarities. The common elements present in all three accounts are patterned in a similar way in each so that an outline of the pattern of action shared by all three can be summed up in a single chart.

(a) The religious hero (or representative) enters distant, foreign land.

(b) He stops at a well.

(c) The girl(s) come(s) to well.

(d) He does something for girl(s).

(e) The girl(s) return(s) home and reports what happened.

(f) The stranger is brought to the household of the girl(s).

(g) Subsequently, it is reported that a marriage occurs between the stranger at the well (or the person for whom he is acting) and the girl (one of the girls) at the well.

Not only are basic elements of the stories similar (the main actor in a foreign land, the well, girl or girls coming to the well, action benefiting the girl or girls, report home, invitation home) but these elements form a general pattern which represents the basic movement of the action in all three stories. Beyond this, there are further similarities which are shared by only two of the three stories. In Genesis 29 and Exodus 2, the main actor is a religious hero, while in Genesis 24 a servant appears as a representative. Jacob and Moses are both fugitives in a strange land, having been forced to leave home because of something they have done. Of course, this is only known about Jacob from a tradition outside the present episode. On the other hand, the Genesis stories are alike in three important ways. The strange land is the old homeland. The girl is a relative. Laban is the one who comes out to meet the stranger. In the Exodus story, the marriage is not so strongly tied to the meeting at the well since seven girls appear and none is identified by name. At the same time, each story has its own character. Genesis 24 is the longest, and so is filled out with more details, events, and even repetitions.

Here again, one might see the stability and flexibility of a tradition of oral prose transmission and suggest that we have an example of a traditional episode which has been employed in and adapted to different contexts. This is at least a possible, although not necessary, conclusion. Some support may be given to an explanation from oral transmission from the way in which the relationships between stories criss-cross. It could be argued that the story of Genesis 29 starts out more like the Exodus story but ends up more like Genesis 24. The other explanations discussed in the previous example cannot be ruled out.

C. *A Visitation in the Wilderness*
(Genesis 16:6-14, Genesis 21:14-19, I Kings 19:4-8)

These three scenes depict the intrusion into the human realm of a heavenly messenger who comes to an outcast or fugitive in the wilderness. The scene from Kings is not a very close parallel, and so it will be discussed after the two Genesis stories have been dealt with.

With regard to the Genesis stories, the similarity extends back into the preceding scene in the sense that the patriarch's wife is the cause of Hagar's departure in both cases, although the details are quite different. In Genesis 16, Sarai complains to Abram that Hagar, having become pregnant, looks down on her mistress. Abram gives her a free hand. She abuses Hagar so that Hagar runs away. In Genesis 21, it is simply said that Sarah noticed Isaac and Ishmael playing together and demanded that Abraham drive Hagar and her son out. Abraham is reluctant until he receives divine approval.

The essential similarities of the two scenes involving Hagar in the wilderness can be set out roughly as follows:

Genesis 16:6-14	*Genesis 21:14-19*
Hagar, pregnant, ran away to wilderness.	Hagar with baby son sent away and went to wilderness.
Beside spring.	
	Finished water and put baby under a bush expecting death.
Messenger intervened. (Instruction: return and promise about son). Promise about son.	Messenger intervened. Instruction: carry on. Promise about son.
Named the spring.	
	Messenger opened her eyes to see spring and she gave son water to drink.

Some commentators have felt an unevenness in the text at verses 9 and 10 of Genesis 16 and proposed that these verses have come in at later stages of the editorial process (for example, Gunkel, 1910:184). Since this proposal is at least a possibility, the instruction given Hagar by the messenger to return and the first of the two promises about her son should be bracketed. This would mean that the points of similarity associated with the intervention of the messenger should perhaps be limited to two: the intervention of the messenger itself and the promise about the son.

The points of difference between the two scenes are fairly obvious. In the first Hagar runs away herself, while in the second she is driven out. In the first story, Hagar is pregnant but in the second she has her baby son with her. The spring is mentioned in both stories but functions differently in each. In Genesis 16, the messenger found Hagar beside a spring. After the promise is given, she gives the spring a name which supposedly reflects the incident. In Genesis 21, the lack of water produces a crisis: the death of the child and possibly the death of Hagar as well although this last is not explicit. The messenger intervenes with words of encouragement, the force of which might be taken as an instruction to carry on. A promise is given concerning the son. Then the messenger responds to the crisis by enabling Hagar to see a spring from which she is able to draw water for her child to drink.

Thus, for the two Hagar stories, the outline of the action common to both is very short and rather general.

(a) Hagar flees or is driven out to the wilderness from Abram (Abraham) with Sarai (Sarah) as instigator.

(b) Messenger intervenes with promise about son.

The scene in I Kings 19:4-8 concerns a prophet who is fleeing for his life. He has gone into the wilderness and sat down under a tree. In the depths of despair, he pleads with Yahweh to take his life. No answer comes from Yahweh. The prophet falls asleep. Then, a divine messengar awakens him with the instruction that he should eat. Food and drink are found at his head. The supernatural appearance is repeated once again except that the instruction to eat a second time is accompanied by a reference to an exhausting journey which lies ahead. After eating, the prophet sets outs on his journey.

This scene from Kings has a general similarity with the two scenes from Genesis. A fugitive or outcast ends up in the wilderness where a divine messenger intervenes to provide support. The degree of likeness is indeed interesting but perhaps not enough to force one to the conclusion that a necessary connection exists. It is at least possible that the Elijah story and the Genesis stories were using a stock scene which was a traditional element in oral composition which was adaptable to various situations in legends.

The striking similarity of the Genesis stories still seems to require some explanation. As with the wife-sister stories, Van Seters argues, with some plausibility, that the account in Genesis 21 is a literary composition which has drawn on Genesis 16 for some of its material (1975:196-202). On the other hand, it seems difficult to rule out the possibility that oral variants may be the basic reason for two rather similar stories. Of course, this does not exclude creativity on the part of the scribe or redactor who produced the present version of the two stories.

D. *A Boy Restored to Life*
(I Kings 17:17-24 and II Kings 4:18-37).

From this point on, all the examples are cases where two stories or scenes are alike. Here, we have two narratives about the death of a boy and his restoration to life through the intervention of a prophet. The two stories are very similar in detail, although the prophet performing the miracle is Elijah in one case and Elisha in the other.

I Kings 17:17-24	*II Kings 4:18-37*
Boy died, son of woman in whose house prophet was staying.	Boy died, son of woman in whose house prophet often stayed.
Woman confronted prophet with reproach.	Woman travelled secretly to prophet utters reproach.

Prophet took boy to his upper room and put him on bed. (He and the boy are apparently alone.)	Prophet entered his room where boy had been put on bed earlier by mother. He and boy are alone with door shut.
Prophet stretched out on boy and prayed.	Prophet prayed and lay on top of boy.
Boy came to life.	Boy opened eyes.
Prophet brought boy back to woman.	Prophet called woman to get son.
Woman confessed that he was a true man of God.	Woman fell at his feet.

While correspondences are not in each case exact, they are extremely close. Furthermore, the points listed above seem to represent the basic outline of the story so that one could say that the two versions share a basic outline like the following.

(a) Son of woman in whose house prophet stays dies.

(b) Woman faces prophet with reproach.

(c) In his room alone with the boy, prophet prays and performs an action which involves lying on the boy.

(d) The boy comes back to life.

(e) Boy is restored to his mother.

(f) Mother responds positively to the prophet.

It is also important to see how the stories are different. The Elisha story is about twice as long as the Elijah story. The Elijah story is spare, recounting the essentials without much elaboration. While the Elisha story has the same essential framework as the short Elijah account, the Elisha narrative has been expanded by elaboration at every point. For example, the sickness of the boy is not simply reported but presented in a brief scene accompanied by dialogue. We know where the illness occurs, what the boy said, and the father's instructions to take the boy to the mother upon whose knees he dies. Then too, when the woman confronts the prophet with the bad news in the Elisha story, the process involves a number of scenes. First the mother puts the boy in the prophet's room. Then she makes preparations to leave. This involves a conversation with her husband from whom she conceals the death of the boy and the purpose of her journey. Next, there is a brief scene in which the prophet sees the woman approaching and sends Gehazi to meet her. But she reveals nothing to him. Then, in a short scene she meets the prophet to utter her reproach. As a result, Gehazi is told what to do and sent with the prophet's staff to deal with the situation. However, the woman persists so that the prophet soon sets out himself. On the way they meet Gehazi returning with the report of his failure. Finally the prophet takes over himself. The healing scene in the Elisha story is also furnished with a few more details. All in all, the fact that the Elisha story is much longer than the Elijah story is due not to a change in the basic plot outline which the two stories share but to the expansion of basic elements listed in the above chart, and especially the second item, the woman's confronting the prophet.

To be sure, the preceding discussion has been restricted. The aim was limited. The purpose of the charts was to provide handy visual illustrations of how the two stories resemble each other. The basic outline giving six basic steps to the story is meant to display only the *common* outline, that is, the outline which emerges when these two stories are set side by side. There may be other valid ways of setting down the pattern of action or structure of these stories when they are taken individually, although the outline does seem to cover the main movements in the plot of each of the versions.

The two stories are so similar that some sort of connection must be assumed. But the nature of this connection cannot be established with certainty. Again, one cannot discount direct borrowing at a written stage when writers may still have had the freedom to adapt and compose. However, the phenomenon of the two versions also fits an oral situation in which a story being transmitted in an unfixed form became attached to different prophets. It might be argued further that the comparison of the two versions shows that the longer story has simply expanded a basic outline largely by the addition of scenes and episodes. This was described above when it was pointed out that the action of the woman coming to the prophet was stated very briefly in the shorter account but spun out through a series of short scenes in the longer version. This kind of expansion was seen to be a normal method of expanding stories in the unfixed method of oral transmission of prose. But would this not occur also in a written tradition? Alexander Rofé claims to see a difference between the shorter and longer stories about the prophets (1970). He argues that the shorter stories betray their popular origin and are close to oral transmission (430-33). The present form is a written condensation (432-33). Rofé suggests that the longer stories, his example being the story in II Kings 4, show a penetrating "discernment of the human soul" (434) and thus must be literary elaborations by a literary genius. While the stories may have resulted from different kinds of literary activity, there is some question as to whether quality can be taken as a clear mark of literary origin.

E. *An Opportunity to Kill the King*
   (I Samuel 23:14-24:23 and I Samuel 26:1-25)

This example is most interesting and requires a very full chart to display the similarities and differences.

I Samuel 23:14-24:23	*I Samuel 26:1-25*
David in wilderness of Ziph. Saul looking for him. Meeting with Jonathan.	
Ziphites went up *to Saul in Gibeah saying: Is not David hiding himself* with us in the fastnesses at Horesh *at the hill of Hachilah*, which is to the south of *Jeshimon?*(23:19)	*Ziphites* came *to Saul in Gibeah saying: Is not David hiding himself at the hill of Hachilah* overlooking *Jeshimon?* (26:1)
Saul asks for further reports. Saul starts search but returns to deal with Philistine threat. David goes to En-gedi. (24:1)	

Saul took *3000 men chosen* from all *Israel*.	*Saul* arose and went down to the wilderness of Ziph and with him were *3000 men chosen* ones of *Israel*.
Saul came into cave where David is without knowing it.	David and Abishai entered Saul's camp and find Saul lying asleep.
David's men urged David to make use of opportunity reminding him that Yahweh had said: See I am going to give *your enemy into your hands*. (24:5)	Abishai said: Today God has delivered *your enemy into your hands*. (26:8)
David cut corner of Saul's garment. David sorry he has done this.	
David said to his men: *Yahweh forbid* that I should do this thing to my Lord, to Yahweh's anointed by *sending out my hand against* him for he is *Yahweh's anointed*. (24:7)	David said to Abishai: do not put an end to him for who has *sent out his hand against Yahweh's anointed . . . Yahweh forbid* from *sending out my hand against Yahweh's anointed*.
	David took Saul's spear and water jug.
Saul left cave.	David and Abishai left camp, unharmed because deep sleep from Yahweh had fallen on camp.
	David called to Abner and reproached for lack of watchfulness. Asked about spear and water jug.
(parallel to this item is below)	Saul recognized voice: *is that your voice, David, my son?*
David called to Saul. Saul looked back. David bowed.	
David said: why . . . listen to men speaking against me? Not true and corner of garment offered as proof of fact that David did not kill Saul in cave. Did not and will not act against king. After whom *has King gone out?* . . . After a dead dog, *a* single *flea?*	*David said: why . . .* pursuing? If Yahweh has set you against me, . . . but if men, cursed are they before Yahweh. . . . for *king has gone out* to look for *a flea*.

Saul said: *is that your voice, David, my son?*	(parallel to this item is above)
Saul admitted he was in the wrong.	Saul admitted that he has sinned. David offered to give spear back.
Saul conceded David would be king and had him swear not to cut off Saul's descendants.	Saul blesses David.
Saul went home. David and his men moved on.	David went his way and Saul returned.

A few comments are required. The first has to do with a small problem in a section of the first narrative, I Samuel 24:5-7. David's men remind him of Yaweh's promise that Yahweh will deliver David's enemy into his hands so that he will be able to do what he wishes (24:5). These words seem to bear the implication that David should kill Saul. However, what follows in the text is David's cutting the corner of Saul's garment (24:5b,6). Consequently, one is led to take this action as David's response to the urging of his men, even though the words of his men appeared to imply that David should kill Saul. It is then stated that David immediately regrets cutting off the corner of the garment. However, in verses 7 and 8, David expresses a strong aversion to any act against Saul and from the way this statement is phrased it appears to be a refusal to follow the urging of David's men, who apparently want their leader to kill Saul. Even if verses 5-7 are ambiguous as they stand, a later speech of David indicates how they must be understood in the present form of the narrative. In verses 10-16, a speech of David to Saul returns to matters described in verses 5-7. The corner of Saul's garment is exhibited as proof that he was close enough to Saul to have killed him but did not. This asserts the view, not entirely clear from the present text of verses 5-7, that the corner of the garment was taken to be used as proof at a later stage and that the action suggested by David's men was murder and it was understood this way by David as well.

There may be room for argument about where the stories begin. The story in I Samuel 26 starts with the Ziphites reporting to Saul who responds immediately with an expedition of 3000 men. It is during this expedition that David enters his camp. In I Samuel 23, there is also a report from the Ziphites to which Saul responds. However, he must give this up and return home because of a Philistine threat. In the meantime, David goes to En-gedi. When this is reported to Saul he goes out again, this time with 3000 men. Thus, one might argue that this episode starts at the beginning of chapter 24 with David's move to En-gedi and the subsequent report of this to Saul. However, it is taken here that the story begins in chapter 23 since the parallels start in this chapter and since the report of David's whereabouts at the beginning of chapter 24 follows naturally from Saul's earlier request for information on David's activities (but see Grønbaek, 1971:156ff).

While the central event in each story is quite different in detail, the incident in the cave and the camp adventure perform the same function in each story. They provide a situation in which the life of Saul is placed in David's hands. Despite urging to take advantage of the situation, David refuses to act against Saul. Consequently, a single outline can be drawn up which represents the outline held in common by the two narratives.

(a) Ziphites report to Saul where David is.
(b) Saul sets out with 3000 chosen men.
(c) Unknowingly Saul lands in a situation where he is at the mercy of David.
(d) David urged by supporter(s) to take advantage of the situation.
(e) David declines on the ground that it is wrong to take action against Yahweh's anointed.
(f) David takes something belonging to Saul without his knowing it.
(g) Saul and David separate.
(h) David calls to Saul. Protests his innocence of any evil intention toward Saul. Something belonging to Saul is offered as proof of David's opportunity to kill Saul.

(i) Saul admits that he is in the wrong.

(j) Saul affirms David's future success.

(k) David and Saul go their own way.

This outline requires some explanation. The actions listed are in a slightly different order in each story. The action in which David surreptitiously takes something belonging to Saul, point (f) above, occurs in different places. However, it has already been noted that I Samuel 23:5-7, where this element is found, is different. Thus, the order of events in the second narrative has been followed. This difference is not taken here as a crucial point against the claim of a common structure. It is more important to see if elements in a different position in parallel stories function in the same way.

Then too, the stories are slightly different at point (h). In I Samuel 26, David first calls to Abner in order to reproach him for his failure to guard the king well. It is at this point that David asks about the spear and water jug. The mention of the spear and water jug in this context of reproach differs from the other account in which the piece of garment is shown directly to Saul as proof that David could have killed him. Still the same point is made. Both items taken by David function as proof that he was close enough to do great harm.

Finally, there is another small variation at point (h). In the first story point (h) involves a single speech by David to Saul. In the other story, the same material is put into two speeches, one to Abner and one to Saul. From the point of view of common structure, the difference in the number of speeches, in the persons addressed, and in the order of contents are not critical since what David has to say at this juncture in both stories is essentially the same thing.

In these two narratives, the similarities are so striking that some kind of relationship has to be assumed. Two extremely interesting features need to be mentioned. First, it was seen that the central incident in each story is different, although the framework of the two stories is much the same. This is not a stock episode in the normal sense, but does this sort of thing not happen in oral transmission? There is stability in some details and wording as well as in the general nature of the story (opportunity to kill the king refused). Flexibility is seen in the fact that the two stories are different. The other remarkable feature is the surprisingly high amount of identical wording. One thinks immediately of borrowing or copying. But how does one account for the fact that the central incidents are not at all alike? Koch mentions Caspari's attempt to explain the similar phrasing as the work of editors trying to make the stories more alike, although Koch himself asks if the reverse might not be true (1969:142, n.12). The field studies of Part I were not specific enough on the matter of fixed phrasing to permit any conclusions to be drawn as to the extent to which this might reflect oral transmission. It is interesting to note that Gunn's recent study (1974) offers examples of Hebrew patterns which contain similar language. On the other hand, Sandmel argues that here we have another example of a haggadist retelling a story, in this case to express his hostility to Saul (1961:114).

F. *Welcome of Strangers*
(Genesis 18:1-8 and Genesis 19:1-3)

These two scenes are now connected in a series of events culminating in the destruction of Sodom and the deliverance of Lot. Of the three figures mentioned in the first account, two continue on to Sodom to save Lot.

Genesis 18:1-8	*Genesis 19:1-3*
	Two men came to Sodom.
Abraham *was sitting* at door of tent.	Lot *was sitting* at gate of Sodom.
He look up, saw three men standing.	
He *saw*, ran *to meet* . . . , *bowed to the ground.*	Lot *saw*, rose *to meet*, *bowed . . . to the ground.*
Offered hospitality (*He said*: *My lord* (*s*) . . . *Wash your feet* . . .); rest and food.	Offered hospitality (*He said* . . . *my lords* . . . *Wash your feet* . . .): to spend the night.

	They refused but Lot urged.
They accepted.	They accepted.
Abraham prepared food.	Lot prepared food.
They ate.	*They ate.*

These were described above as scenes. This is perhaps not strictly accurate because in each case the narrative following these sections continues without a change of setting or without any significant lapse of time. Nevertheless, they do seem to represent a recognizable segment or stage in the narrative. The strangers appear, an invitation is issued, and it is accepted. The visitors are brought together with the main character. What follows in each case is a new segment of the narrative. In the Abraham story, there is an announcement of a son to Sarah and her response to this news. In the Lot story, the men of Sodom appear with their demand.

These two segments are similar but again it is difficult to say how this has come about. One might argue that the action portrayed here was the sort of thing which happened time after time in real life, and so it would be perfectly natural for narratives to reflect what usually happened when strangers were invited. Still, we know from the larger narrative context that the strangers are far from ordinary passers-by. The scenes in question both appear to perform a definite function in the larger narrative since they set the stage for a more important action. Thus, there is some justification for entertaining the possibility that this is a case of a stock scene or episode used in oral narrative composition. One can point to both stability and flexibility. On the one hand, the similarity is close, even to wording which is almost identical (italicized in chart above). On the other hand, the scene is adapted to different settings involving invitations of a different kind. Nevertheless, these two scenes are in such close proximity that the possibility of a deliberate repetition for artistic purposes in oral or even written composition is very real. Again, no single explanation emerges as unavoidable.

G. *Guests Are Insulted*
(Genesis 19:4-11 and Judges 19:22-25).

The demarcation of these stories needs some comment. The beginning of each of these episodes is clearly marked in the sense that the trouble starts in each with the appearance of the men of the city. Some of the wording in the opening sentence is identical: "the men of the city. . . surrounded the house." The ending of the episode in the Sodom story, in Genesis 19, is clear because the matter of the men of the city is finished in verse 11. Attention is then directed to something else, namely getting Lot and his family out of the doomed city. It is not as easy, however, to draw a clear line at the end of the end of the story in Judges 19. If the demand made by the men of the city is from the point of view of plot a problem which needs to be solved, at what point is this problem solved? Here, verse 25 has been taken as the end of the episode because the problem is in a sense solved when the unfortunate concubine is pushed out the door. At least, the attention of the men of the city is distracted from the guest whom they had demanded in the first instance. However, the next stage in the Judges narrative is the discovery of the dead concubine at the door next morning. Now, of course, this is very closely related to what precedes since it seems to represent the crowning point of the insult which then demanded retribution. That is to say, if the concubine had not died, the action of the men of the city, gross as it was, may not have demanded the punishment which occcupies the subsequent stages of the narrative. Since the precise division of the text into segments is not at stake here, the matter of where the episode ends need not be resolved. At verse 25, the parallel with the Sodom story ends and so it is convenient to stop here for purposes of comparision.

Genesis 19:4-11	Judges 19:22-25
Men of the city . . . surrounded house. Where are the men who came? *Bring* them *out* to us *so that we may know* them.	*Men of the city . . . surrounded house.* *Bring out* the man who came *so that we may know him.*

Host *went out . . . and said* : *My brothers, do not do wrong. See, my daughters . . . I will bring them out* for you. *Do what you want* to them *but do not do anything to these men.*	Host *went out . . . and said* No, *my brothers, do not do wrong . . . See, my daughter . . . I will bring her out . . . do what you want but do not do* this foolish *thing to the man.*
Men refused and began to break in.	The men refused.
Guests pulled Lot in and shut door. They struck men outside with blindness so that they could not find the door.	The guest pushed his concubine outside so that the men are occupied with her until morning.

The similarities are quite obvious in the first three elements in the above chart, but the fourth element is different as far as content is concerned. In the Genesis story, the guests bring supernatural power to bear causing blindness; in the Judges story, the guest takes action and saves the situation, at least for himself and his host. However, even though these last elements may be different in content, they are the same from the point of view of function. The miracle on the one hand and the action of the guest on the other both solve the problem presented in the first element, a threat by the men of the city to the guests. A brief statement of the common outline shared by the two episodes might look like the following.

(a) The men of the city surround the house. Demand: bring out the guest(s) so that we may know them.

(b) Host appeals: My brothers, do not do wrong. See, my daughter(s) . . . I will bring her (them) out . . . do what you want but do not do anything to the man (men).

(c) Men refuse.

(d) Guest(s) act(s) to save the situation.

Here again, it is difficult to offer a single, obvious explanation for the striking similarity of these two episodes. In the first two elements, the similarity is especially close because much of the wording is the same. Although the charts given in these examples are not intended to be a translation, the restatement of the contents was given more fully to show the similarity in wording.

Italicization identifies phrases which are virtually identical. Yet with all the similarity, the last element is quite different. That this key action should be different can be viewed in association with the persons who fill the role of the guests. In the Lot story, the guests are no ordinary mortals and are able to bring supernatural power into play. In the other story, the guest has little more than his wits with which to defend himself, even though his solution does not entirely satisfy modern readers. This is the third instance of an example in which close similarity in wording has been noted. What was said about these previous examples would apply here as well, except that a stronger case can be developed here for literary imitation.

The similarities between Genesis 19 and Judges 19 extend beyond the episodes under discussion. The Lot story is preceded by a scene in which strangers are welcomed. This scene has already been discussed in the previous example where it was set beside a remarkably similar scene in Genesis 18. In the Genesis narrative, Lot is sitting in the square of the city. When the two strangers come, he persuades them to stay at his house, all of which prepares for the attempted attack on the guests. In Judges, the scene directly preceding the attempted assault on the guest is also a scene in which hospitality is offered to a stranger, although it was not close enough to the two Genesis stories to be included in the previous example. Nevertheless, the similarities between the Lot story and Judges are quite significant, except that in Judges 19 the stranger is the one who sits in the square and it is the future host who passes by. This additional point of contact between Genesis 19 and Judges 19 might lend support to an argument for direct dependence of one story on the other.

Indeed, reasons for deliberate imitation can be proposed. It could be urged that the story of Judges 19 deliberately follows the structure and even wording of the Sodom story in Genesis 19 in order to suggest a parallel between the wickedness of the men of Gibeah and to make the subsequent punishment of the Benjaminites by the rest of Israel appear all the more deserved. Although less likely on the face of it, the reverse hypothesis might be tested: crime of Gibeah achieved archetypal status by being used as the model for an episode in the Sodom story.

It is not necessary to work out all possible explanations for the close likeness of Genesis 19 and Judges 19. What has been said so far is sufficient to indicate the nature of the problem of comparing these two blocks of material. A quick glance at the commentaries and standard introductions is sufficient to indicate the wide range of proposals made by scholars (for example, Burney, 1970:442ff., also Albright's brief comments in the prolegomenon to this reprint, 24f.). In view of the complexity of the relationship between the two episodes being compared here, only one point needs to be made. It might still be possible to argue that the similarity is due to the use of a standard episode from a traditional stock of commonly used material in oral narration of prose with no direct dependence or imitation. But before such a proposal could be considered the best explanation, many questions would have to be answered and many things explained, especially the matters discussed above which tend to support a theory of conscious imitation.

H. *Visit of a Messenger*
   (Judges 6:11-24 and Judges 13:2-24).

These two episodes might appear at first glance to be quite different. One tells about the announcement of the birth of Samson to his parents; the other describes the call of Gideon to save Israel. However, apart from the specific content of the different messages, both episodes relate the appearance of a messenger of Yahweh who delivers a message and the reaction of the person or persons to whom the message is delivered.

Judges 6: 11-24	*Judges 13: 2-24*
Messenger of Yahweh came and sat under tree, Gideon threshing wheat. Messenger of Yahweh appeared to him.	Wife of Manoah was childless. Messenger of Yahweh appeared to her.

Messenger said: Yahweh is with you, Gideon suggested opposite is true, Yahweh (?) said: save Israel from Midian!

Messenger said: you will have a son. Bring him up as a Nazirite. He will start to save Israel from the Philistines.

Gideon objected: how possible? Yahweh replied: I will be with you.

Gideon asked for a sign and proposed that he bring an offering.

Woman reported to husband. Manoah asked Yahweh to send man again. Messenger of Yahweh came again, this time to Manoah and wife, and repeated instructions about upbringing of boy. Manoah offered food. Messenger countered with suggestion of an offering.

Manoah asked Messenger's name. Messenger refused.

Gideon prepared kid and cakes. Told to put it on a rock.

Manoah took the kid and meal offering.

Messenger touched food with staff. Fire sprang up. Messenger disappeared.

Manoah offered them upon rock. When flame went up, Messenger went up in flame.

Gideon saw that he was a messenger of Yahweh.

Manoah and wife saw and fell to ground. Manoah knew that he was a messenger of Yahweh.

Gideon cried out in despair at having seen a Messenger of Yahweh. Yahweh assured him that he would not die.

Manoah expressed fear to wife that that they will die because they saw God. Wife suggested that this is not likely.

Gideon built altar there.

Woman had a son.

Significant problems arise out of some scholarly discussion of these texts. This will be picked up at a later point. These two texts will first be examined as they stand in order to get a general view of the similarities in both content and structure. The similarity in content is the closest in the events surrounding the offering. In both episodes, it is determined that an offering should be brought, and the offering in each case involves a kid. In both episodes, a miraculous occurence is associated with the fire at the offering. The messenger of Yahweh who comes to Gideon produces fire when he touches the offering with his staff. While Manoah's fire is not the result of a miracle, the messenger of Yahweh disappears into the flame. The miracle establishes the true nature of the messenger and the validity of his message. The immediate response is the recognition of the person as a messenger of Yahweh. This is followed by a fear of death because the meeting with the messenger has brought them into contact with the divine. While it was said above that the announcement delivered by the messenger was different in each case, a certain parallel does exist in that Gideon is told to save Israel from Midian and the son announced to Manoah and his wife will make a start at saving Israel from the Philistines.

As far as structure is concerned, the course of action held in common by the two episodes can be summarized in the following chart.

(a) Messenger appears.

(b) He delivers his message, having to do with saving Israel.

(c) An offering is proposed and brought.

(d) Miraculous occurrence is associated with the fire of the offering, and messenger disappears.

(e) The participant(s) now know(s) that he is a messenger of Yahweh.

(f) Fear of death is expressed.

(g) Assurance comes that there is nothing to fear.

Perhaps another element should be added which is clear in the Gideon account but less so in the other. Gideon asks for a sign as a decisive confirmation of the message. The subsequent miracle apparently offers this. In the other story, there is no specific request for a sign, although the husband does ask for the man to return arguing that he needs to know how to bring the child up. But this information was already given to the wife at the first meeting. However, if the husband's request has something to do with his doubt about the authenticity of the message, then perhaps the husband is displaying a desire for corroboration which amounts to a request for a sign. The return of the messenger and the associated miraculous happening could then be seen as the response to Manoah's implied request for a sign. But all this is not clear from Judges 13 and so it was not included in the chart.

So far, one might argue as in previous examples that the similarities and differences evident here might reflect the stability and flexibility of a stock episode or description in oral transmission applied to two different contexts. However, scholars have not been in agreement about the unity of Judges 6. Wolfgang Richter (1966:122-55) has presented full and detailed arguments for the presence of two sources in this chapter. For him, Judges 6:11a, 18f, 21-4 is an older story centered on the statement of Yahweh in verse 23, with an altar aetiology added at a later point. On the other hand, Richter argues that 11b-17 is a story constructed and inserted here by the writer who produced the "*Retterbuch*" of Judges 6-9. Richter does not discover sources in . Judges 13 but sees it as a combination of motifs from Genesis 18 and Judges 6. He is not arguing for literary dependence but rather an instance of a very full unfolding of traditional motifs by an author who has tried to produce an appropriate beginning to the Samson stories. The arguments in support of these proposals are rather extensive and spread into several other chapters of biblical material. There will be no attempt to test the validity of Richter's arguments here. On the face of it, Richter's suggestions about Judges 6 and 13 are plausible, although perhaps not inevitable. As seen above, it is possible to sketch out an argument for the presence of a stock description in these two chapters which may have had its origin in a tradition of oral transmission, although this argument may not be particularly compelling in this case.

While the tendency has been to avoid examples about which there has been considerable scholarly debate about the sources, this pair of stories was tentatively included because Richter's discussion itself raises some valuable questions. If Richter is correct, then we are dealing with written and not oral compositions and the overall structures of Judges 6:11-24 and

13:2-14 are literary rather than examples of a stock description. But, as Richter points out, the elements which make up these chapters, the "motifs," are traditional and thus likely oral in origin. It was seen in Part I that building narratives with the use of smaller traditional elements, or building blocks, was an essential part of the kind of oral prose transmission described there. Thus it is unlikely that the kind of combination of motifs that Richter sees in these chapters began with writing. There is a question which needs further serious examination. Even if Judges 6 and 13 are the product of authors using writing, will the method of composition by means of combining traditional elements be radically different from what was known in oral transmission where so much of this material must have originated?

I. *The Prophet and the Wonderful Vessel*
(I Kings 17:7-16 and II Kings 4:1-7)

This is another example of a similar story being found in the Elijah and Elisha narratives. The Elisha story appears to be more of a self-contained unit than the Elijah account which is more closely integrated into the narrative context. The Elijah story is the second of two episodes following the announcement of the famine. Both episodes are closely related to the famine announcement because they are illustrations of how Yahweh looked after the prophet in difficult times. In the first, the prophet is sent to a wadi where he drinks of the water and is fed by birds. In I Kings 17:7, it is reported that the wadi dried up because of the lack of rain. This statement announces a new condition requiring further divine action to keep the prophet alive, and so this verse is taken as the beginning of the episode.

There is no point in producing charts in this instance because these two stories do not have a common structure except in the sense that a problem emerges in each which is then solved by the intervention of the prophet with a miracle. This difference in structure will be discussed at a later point (see examples 7 and 9 in Part III). The obvious similarity lies in two main areas of content.

In each story, a widow has a problem involving a lack, food in the one case and money in the other. The solution to the problem entails the action of a prophet through a vessel or vessels which miraculously keep producing flour and oil.

It is possible to see in these two stories stability and change which might come from oral transmission. Here, the stability can be seen in the two items of content mentioned above, the widow in need and the action with a vessel or vessels. The change can be seen in the different framework that each story has developed. But here again, an explanation in terms of oral tradition is not the only possibility. It is worth noting that in both the Elijah and Elisha traditions, the story about the boy restored to life follows the story about the widow and the miraculous vessel(s). One might argue that creative scribal activity reproduced similar stories for the prophetic tradition which lacked them so that both prophets would appear capable of the same kinds of actions. Alternatively, the explanation of oral transmission would see versions of the story becoming attached to each prophetic tradition in the oral period.

CONCLUDING COMMENTS

This investigation of similar episodes and stories was viewed as an opportunity to do two things: to consider the phenomenon of repeated elements of narrative in the light of the discussion of oral prose and use these stories to inquire further about similarity.

It was anticipated from the start that an investigation from the point of view of the nature of oral prose would not lead to very definite conclusions. Two major difficulties were indicated. The total amount of material is small compared to the large amounts available to folklorists and students of oral literature. In addition, most of the nine examples used are cases of only two occurrences. The examination of the nine examples itself produced a varied picture. In some cases, the parallel stories had items of content in common, that is, the same or very similar actors, actions, and other details, but no common framework: A (wife-sister), C

(Hagar), and I (miraculous vessel). Others had both items of content and a framework in common: B (well), D (restoring the boy), F (welcome of strangers), G (insult), H (visit of messenger), although the degree and kind of similarity as to contents and framework varied. One example, E (David and Saul), consisted of two different stories with quite different content which nevertheless shared a common general framework. Finally, the phenomenon of a significant amount of identical or close to identical wording was noted in examples E, F, and G. Following the rather general clue from Part I that something like stock scenes and episodes are a characteristic of orally composed prose, I have suggested that many of the nine examples could be stock or traditional material. They also reflect the stability and flexibility to be expected in the kind of transmission of oral prose described in Part I in that the material appears to be adapted to different contexts and changed according to the interests of different narrators. There is here, perhaps, the danger of turning difficulties into virtues by explaining differences as well as similarities as evidence of oral transmission.

While it was argued that the evidence appeared to be compatible with what might be expected in orally composed prose, it was conceded that the alternative suggestion of literary imitation in a scribal tradition, as suggested by Van Seters, could not be ruled out. We do not know enough about oral style or scribal style to be able to decide clearly for one or the other. At this point, however, we should ask whether the choice may be reduced simply to one or the other. It would seem that between the two extremes of oral and written there lies a range of possibilities to be considered. The first thing to be done is to exclude the two extremes. Strictly speaking, oral means performance. Once oral tradition is written down changes occur and the most that could be said about biblical texts is that they may bear a very close relationship to oral tradition. On the other side, scholars today know what a well developed literary tradition is because they live in one. We experience biblical literature as different from our own in many ways. Thus, if we speak of biblical material as literary or written, we would have to keep in mind that it is closer in time to a period of traditional oral literature and so may still bear a relationship to or reflect the influence of oral tradition.

This middle area, the spectrum between oral and written, has not been plotted but some suggestions can be made as to the possibilities which need to be taken into account. Normally, texts taken down from oral tradition will reflect oral style very strongly, although the way in which oral poems and stories get written down is a rather complex question (Culley, 1967:23-27). Conceivably, narrative texts taken down could be anything from a very short summary to a fully expanded narrative (but see Rofé, 1970:432-3). On the one hand, there are different kinds of transmitters of oral tradition, ranging from creative to passive (Dégh, 1969:171-2). On the other hand, recorders of oral tradition may well have retold stories so as to reflect their own tastes and interests. If this happens, we may then think of a scribe or recorder as a "performer" recording his version of the traditional narrative or narratives. At first glance, such a text might look very much like a text taken down by dictation from an oral performer. Even authors deliberately composing in writing may continue to use a style which has come from a tradition of oral narrative. This may be seen from the discussions about "transitional" texts among students of oral literature (see, for example, Lord, 1974:200-10). Even in the case of the Icelandic sagas where a work like *Njals saga* may be accepted as the product of an author who had control of his material from beginning to end, some recent scholars are quite prepared to describe the style as oral (Allen, 1971:20-28; Scholes and Kellogg, 1966:43-51). It appears that one need not expect a radical discontinuity between the style of orally composed texts and texts produced by scribes or authors writing in a period close to oral tradition so that it should not be surprising to find a significant level of traditional material including stock scenes and episodes as well as stereotyped language and expressions (Culley, 1967:25-7; Gunn, 1974:311-13). The mode of building narratives in scribal tradition may be an elaborate extension of the mode already developed and established in oral. Finally, as the movement away from oral increases or new genres come into existence in written tradition, the gap between oral style and written style becomes greater.

It is clear then that the problem of oral and written with the whole range of possibilities in between is not a simple one but needs more investigation and discussion, and this is especially true for oral prose. With regard to the nine examples studied above each case was dealt with separately and some attempt was made to comment on the special problems found in each. Perhaps this is as far as the discussion can be carried for the moment.

Apart from the question of oral tradition, the comparison of parallel stories permits a few observations relevant to the problem of structure to be considered in the next part. In the first place, it was seen that different persons could fill the same or similar roles. This was perhaps most noticeable in example A, the wife-sister stories where one patriarch and his wife, or one foreign king, could be changed for the other. In example B, the episode about the meeting at the well, a servant plays the role filled in the other stories by a religious hero, although the servant is acting as a representative of Abraham and Isaac. A similar thing happens with regard to settings. A second feature worth noticing is that different actions can have the same function in different stories. This was mentioned in connection with example A, the wife-sister stories. In the first two accounts, the patriarch's lie about his wife was discovered when the deity revealed the matter to the king, while in the last story the king discovered the deception by accident. Another interesting example of this was seen in G where the guests were insulted. In the Sodom story, the situation was saved when the guests performed a miracle and struck the men of the city blind. In the other story, the guest accomplished the same thing when he threw out his concubine. The most striking example of different actions but similar functions was seen in H, the stories about Saul and David. The stories are different yet follow a similar pattern. David finds himself in a position to kill Saul (cave/camp) but, despite being urged to do so, he declines to murder the king. David takes something belonging to Saul (piece

of garment/spear and water jug) and presents it at a later meeting
with the king. A third phenomenon was seen where two stories
had the same general framework of action yet were of very
different length. A clear example of this can be seen in D, the story
of the boy restored to life, where the first story is less than half as
long as the second. The expansion occurs through the elaboration
of the elements which make up the general framework. In other
words, it was clearly seen that a sentence or two can function in the
same way in a narrative as a more lengthy scene. These three
observations lead directly to the next part in which stories will be
compared according to their plot outlines stated in various
degrees of abstraction.

Part III

Structure in Some Biblical Narratives

While attention has been focused so far on the question of oral transmission of prose and its characteristics, the question of story patterns, and thus narrative structure, has been very prominent as well. In this part, attention will be concentrated primarily on the matter of structure. However, structure will be approached through the discussion of the preceding parts by following some of the clues which came to light there. The patterns which will be discussed may or may not have something to do with oral tradition, but the scope has been broadened from the structure of oral prose narratives to the structure of prose narratives as such, although, just as with the investigation of oral prose, the discussion will be limited to certain aspects of the question.

When comparing parallel texts in the previous part, it was often possible to draw up an outline of the action. This outline was described as the common outline for the two or three scenes or stories being compared. In order to make an outline which could serve as a statement of a common framework of two or three versions of a story or scene, it was often necessary to generalize by speaking of roles instead of specific persons and of events and actions in terms of how they function in a story rather than of the specific activities and happenings related in the narrative. This meant that the different elements in the outline might be at different degrees of generalization or abstraction depending on how closely the stories or scenes being compared resembled each other at various points.

As far as whole stories or scenes are concerned, one can think of several possible degrees of abstraction to which a generalized framework of the action may be carried. For example, the first

story of example D in the previous part (I Kings 17:17-24) tells
how Elijah restored a boy to life. But it was seen that this story and
the story of Elisha in II Kings 4:8-37 shared a fairly specific
framework of common action. The main actors are different and
the second story is more elaborate, but otherwise the similarities
are striking. Now, there are other stories about these two prophets
in which they are approached about a problem and to which they
respond with a miraculous action which solves the problem. Thus,
if the action is stated in this general way, several stories of Elijah
and Elisha, and perhaps Moses as well, share this general pattern
or structure. Further generalization might lead to a pattern
something like: problem/response/problem solved. This would
cover not only the stories just mentioned but also deception
stories in which a deception rather than a miracle solves the
problem (Culley, 1974). Then, it is possible to go even further and
suggest a structure like: problem/problem solved. Very many
stories indeed would share this pattern. Crisis/denouement might
be even more general.

The intention here is not to establish all the possible degrees of
abstraction but merely to indicate briefly that choices are
available. Choice depends on a number of factors. Usefulness is an
important factor to consider, and this in turn is related to the
purpose and scope of a given study. For example, if a pattern is
very specific, the number of stories capable of being brought
under it is apt to be small. Specific patterns were featured in Part
II because there was a particular interest in oral tradition. On the
other hand, a very general description such as problem/problem
solved would involve so many stories that it might have limited
usefulness. In what follows, the level of generalization will be
worked out in terms of the group of stories being examined. As far
as questions of scope and purpose are concerned, an attempt has
already been made to sketch these matters in broad outline
elsewhere (Culley, 1974:165-72). What was said there applies here,
too. There are many ways of looking at structure in narrative texts
and there are many elements in texts which might be taken into
consideration. What follows represents an exploration of one way

of looking at structure by taking a limited number of elements into account.

The biblical material chosen for consideration is a group of narratives which will be referred to as "miracle stories," and only a very few of all those stories in the Old Testament which conceivably might be called miracle stories will be considered. In choosing stories, two characteristics were especially sought: (a) the stories should be as short as possible; and (b) they should be as free as possible from marks which might indicate a combination of sources. Shorter, less complicated items are preferable for the simple reason that they are apt to be easier to handle. Furthermore, the results of an analysis of small units may provide a sound basis for an approach to other more complex biblical narrative material.

No genre definition is implied by the term "miracle story." This term merely provides a useful label for stories in which miracle, here understood as divine intervention to help or to punish, plays a prominent role.

It is recognized that the problems of defining miracle in biblical tradition is more complex than this. However, since defining the nature of miracle in biblical texts is not an issue here, it should not be necessary to pursue the matter further. Divine intervention means quite simply that Yahweh has intervened either directly or through a representative like a prophet to cause something to happen to the advantage or disadvantage of someone. Intervention means that Yahweh causes something to happen that human beings cannot themselves normally cause to happen. It may be bringing water from a rock. It may be having an otherwise normal event like rain stop and start on command.

The choice of a group of miracle stories for a trial analysis offers some advantages. First of all, if a group of stories having miracle as a prominent element are brought together, then there is a good chance that similarities in structure will also be found so that it will be possible to group stories according to structural patterns. Attention is to be focused on the group. Structure will be defined in terms of a specific group of stories. The use of a group will help set the level of generalization or abstraction at which the structure is stated.

A second reason why miracle stories provide good material for this study is that, while these stories vary greatly in length, most are short and some are very short. Stories which are very short will likely contain little more than the essential outline of the narrative. In comparing stories it will be considered legitimate to look for a minimal structure and to speak of essential and non-essential elements in texts. The very short stories will assist in establishing the essential elements, that is, those elements which would have to appear in a reduced, generalized restatement of the structure of a group of stories. All this bears on a problem facing any kind of structural analysis of texts, namely, the problem of segmentation, or how to divide up texts into appropriate components (Voigt, 1972:85). Comparison of shorter and longer stories may assist in determining elements which must be taken into consideration.

At this point, no clearly defined method is being proposed whereby the texts to be considered below may be subjected to a stringently controlled, systematic analysis. The approach is exploratory. Each text will be taken in turn. The discussion will be cumulative aiming at a summing up at the end of this process. Nevertheless, the intention is that the analysis should be descriptive as far as possible. Thus, the strategy is employed of using groups of stories within which there are some very short stories which can serve as minimal units. It is hoped that this will introduce some measure of control into the process.

Seven Examples Where Intervention Comes as Help

1. Elisha Makes Bad Water Good to Drink (11 Kings 2:19-22)

Since this story is short, the action can be conveniently summarized as follows:

19. The men of the city said to Elisha, ". . . the water is bad and the land lacks fertility."
20. He said, "Get me a new dish and put salt in it." They got it for him.
21. He went out . . . threw salt . . . and said, "So says Yahweh, 'I restore . . . no more death and sterility from it.'"
22. And so the waters were restored to a pure state and have remained so to this day, just as the Yahweh word which Elisha had uttered had said.

A minor difficulty is evident and can be commented on immediately. In verse 19, the problem brought to Elisha's attention consists of water and land, but in verses 21 and 22 only the water is mentioned. However, from the point of view of the framework of the story which will be set out below, whether the problem is water and land or just water is not a crucial issue. It will be assumed for the purposes of discussion that water alone constitutes the problem.

Since the story is so short, very little can be removed from the text without essential information being lost about the course of the action in the narrative. Now, it is true that from many points of view everything in a story is essential. All the words and clauses perform some function, and in any case the narrator probably wanted the text as it now stands. But it was decided above that it would be permissible to speak of essential and non-essential elements in texts from the point of view of developing generalized frameworks of the action. Here, the remark made in verse 19 to the effect that the situation or location of the city was good as the prophet himself could see can be considered non-essential. Thus, the story as it stands is very close to a minimal structure except that it is still stated in very specific language which could apply only to this story.

But how can the structure be stated in more general terms? First of all, with regard to the actors, there are two parties. The first party is the men of the city, apparently Jericho. The other party is the prophet, Elisha, and behind him Yahweh whose word and power are brought into play. The interaction between these two parties can be followed easily from the above outline. The men tell Elisha that the water is bad. Thus, a party with a problem, an undesirable situation, draws it to the attention of a person who stands in a special relationship to the deity in that he is able to bring forces from the supernatural realm to bear on undesirable situations and change them. Even though all this is not explicitly said in verse 19, it is implicit in the story since the larger context of the prophet stories make clear what kind of person Elisha is. For the men to bring a problem to his attention amounts to an appeal to him to do something about it. Thus, verse 19 performs the function not only of stating the problem but also of having the party with a problem bring this to the attention of the person close to Yahweh so that he may respond.

The response follows. The first step, verse 20, consists in the prophet giving instructions for certain materials to be brought. When they are brought, Elisha goes out to the spring and does two things. He performs an action with the material and utters a word of Yahweh which announces explicitly that the desired change is taking place. Thus, the response of the prophet involves instruction, action with material, and a divine word announcing the appropriate solution to the problem.

Finally, in verse 22, the fact that the change announced in the word of Yahweh has indeed occurred is stated. The water became good. It is further indicated that the water remained good up to the time of the narrator, with the added reminder that this was as the prophet had announced. This last part confirms the intervention of Yahweh through the prophet with clear, positive results.

Since this story is so short, it is not difficult to propose a generalized statement of the pattern of action even though the other stories in the group have not yet been considered. One of the obvious things to be noted is that this short narrative opens with a statement of a problem situation and closes with the statement of the solution of the problem. And so in a very general sense the movement goes from a problem to the solution of the problem. However, to say that the structure is "problem/problem solved" leaves the description general since the way the problem is solved has significance as well. If the statement of the problem at the beginning of the story constitutes an appeal by the persons touched by the problem to a person who, because of his special relationship to Yahweh, would be able to bring supernatural power into play, then the response of the prophet should be considered an important structural element. It should be considered separate from the outcome of the story where it is indicated that the problem is solved. In this particular story the response takes the form of instructions that some material be obtained which Elisha then uses on the source of the problem. In this case, a word of Yahweh is also pronounced. Finally, the outcome or result of the action taken by the prophet is reported and this report forms at the same time an announcement of the solution to the problem.

Thus the structure of the story, II Kings 2:19-22, can be set out in a brief chart like the following:

(1) A party brings their problem situation to the attention of the prophet.

(2) The prophet responds with instructions to get a material which he then applies to the problem situation along with a word of Yahweh announcing the solution of the problem.

(3) The result of the miraculous intervention accompanying the prophet's response is stated and it is clear that the problem is resolved.

2. Elisha Makes the Poison Stew Good to Eat (II Kings 4:38-41)

This example is also very short but the balance of elements within the story is not the same as in the previous narrative. In the first example, the problem was set out in one verse. In this story, three verses are needed. Verses 38 and 39 describe a background situation leading up to a crisis in verse 40. In verse 38, Elisha is at Gilgal during a time of famine with members of the prophetic order. For some reason, not explained, Elisha orders that a stew be prepared. Some wild gourds are collected and put in the pot.

Apparently, these became a source of danger in the stew. When the stew is poured out, the men are just beginning to eat when trouble is discovered. The problem is brought to the attention of Elisha. Here then, several clauses are devoted to a description of the steps leading up to the problem. This means not only a longer section devoted to the description of the problem as compared with the previous example but also a rather long section as compared with the space given to the following response of the prophet and the result of his action. Why the problem of bad water was introduced so abruptly in the first story while the problem of the bad stew is depicted here in more detail need not detain us. Perhaps bad water was a common enough phenomenon but a bad stew required some explanation. The point to be made is that II Kings 2:19 and II Kings 4:38-40 perform roughly the same function in their respective stories, the description of a problem, even though one is presented briefly and the other in some detail.

The rest of the story can be summarized as was done in the preceding example.

40.   They called out, "Man of God, death is in the pot." And so they could not eat it.

41a. He said, "Get me some meal."
       He threw it into the pot.

   b. He said, "Pour it out for the people so that they can eat it."
       Nothing bad was in the pot.

In verses 40 and 41, there are two parties: a group earlier identified as members of the prophetic order and Elisha, known in other stories as a prophet but here only as a "Man of God." As in the previous example, the group draws the attention of the prophet to a problem situation in which they find themselves. However, there are differences to be noted. For example, the prophet is part of the group and apparently was going to share the stew with the others. But a more important difference is the matter of the bad stew. Can this really be called a problem in the same way that bad water was for the men of Jericho? Since no human answer to the problem of bad water was available to the men of Jericho, the appeal to a prophet for a supernatural answer through Yahweh's intervention was a logical move. On the other hand, bad stew could have been thrown out. Furthermore, the cry which draws the attention of the Man of God to the condition of the stew, if in fact the words mean that the stew was poisoned, could be taken as a warning and so it is not necessary to argue that the cry was an appeal for the prophet to invoke supernatural power to correct the situation. From our point of view at least, the problem of the stew appears to be a minor one. It might be that the poison stew merely provided an occasion for Elisha to demonstrate his ability to call in special powers. This last interpretation must be acknowledged to be a genuine possibility. But, whether the emphasis in one of these narratives is on a genuine situation of human need followed by a compassionate response or on the miraculous response to a minor crisis, the prophet figure seems to do much the same thing. The difference in emphasis would become apparent to the extent that one was confident of being able to distinguish between a minor crisis and a crying need. In any case, there is still here a problem of sorts to which the prophet responds with the result that it is miraculously solved and so the outline for this example runs very much like that of the previous example.

Whatever the precise emphasis the problem of the poison stew be given, Elisha responds. His first reaction is, as in the foregoing story, to give instructions that a material be brought. Just as in the other story, he throws it into the substance which is the source of the difficulty. This time, however, there is no word of Yahweh pronouncing a change. That a miraculous change has taken place is indicated in verse 40b by Elisha's instruction to pour out the stew for the people to eat, along with the added statement that the stew was no longer dangerous.

Now it is true that in verses 38 and 39 there are actors other than the two parties represented by Elisha and the group acting as a whole as in verses 40 and 41. There is the person who is instructed by Elisha to make the stew and another person who went out to get the ingredients, bringing back the wrong ones. Again, however, it is maintained that comparison of examples 1 and 2 indicates clearly enough that verses 38 and 39 display an action which is part of a larger action. Thus, what goes on in verses 38 and 39 can be called subordinate and not on the same level as the actions in the following outline:

(1) A party discovers a problem.
The party brings this to the attention of the prophet.
(2) The prophet responds with instructions to get him a material which he then applies to the problem.
(3) The result of the miraculous intervention accompanying the prophet's response is stated.

If the above outline is a valid one, then a general parallel can be seen with example 1. When examples 1 and 2 are placed side by side, what stands out is the same general structure (but see Long 1973a:496 and 1973b:346-47). A problem comes to the attention of a person standing in a special relationship to Yahweh. This person responds to the problem situation by performing an action involving the use of a material. This action appears to be accompanied by intervention of a supernatural force producing a miraculous change so that the substance creating the problem is changing from bad to good, removing the problem. Close points of similarity can be seen in the throwing of a material into the offending substance. Difference can be seen in the use of a word of Yahweh in one case but no actual reference to the intervention of Yahweh in the other. That such an intervention took place may be inferred from the fact that this story is one of many miracle stories. In the others the intervention of Yahweh is often explicit. In biblical Hebrew narrative, the supernatural intrusion is usually attributed to Yahweh.

3. Through Moses Yahweh Makes Bitter Water Sweet (Exodus 15:22-27)

There is here a problem of literary unity. In examples 1 and 2, the beginning and end of each narrative was clearly marked since what preceded and followed in each case were parts of other stories. Furthermore, it was pointed out that both examples began with the statement of a problem and ended with the removal of that problem. Commenting on the present section, George Coats identifies verse 22a and verse 27 as phrases of a type used by P in the framework of narratives (1968:49). Since both of these verses announce movement from one place to another, they are not of crucial relevance to the kind of analysis being done here, although they may well be important markers if analysis is carried out at other levels. Another complication arises from Coats's comment that verses 25b and 26 are deuteronomistic (but see Childs 1974:266f.). This could be sufficient grounds for bracketing them out of the present discussion. Even without reference to source analysis, however, these verses could be relegated to a secondary level in that their presence does not modify the pattern of action in the miracle story. They appear to be commenting on the story or using the story to make a point. It is worth considering that the miracle story plus comment may itself be a pattern which could be paralleled in other places. But to pursue this possibility goes beyond the scope of the present study. Thus, from more than one point of view it appears legitimate to restrict discussion to verses 22b to 25a. Even within these verses it has been suggested that there is tension between 22b and 23 but since verse 22b can be taken as background leading up to verse 23, this possibility will be ignored (Coats, 1968:48).

This story is again very short and can be summarized as follows:

22b. They went . . . but did not find water.

23. They came to Marah but could not drink the water because it was bitter. This is why it is called Marah.

24. The people complained to Moses, saying, "What will we drink."

25. He cried out to Yahweh. Yahweh showed him a piece of wood. He threw it into the water. The water became sweet.

In this brief narrative, the problem situation introduced at the beginning is serious. In territory where water is hard to find at the best of times, the only water found is undrinkable. The presence of a naming element at this point has led to the proposal that verse 23 is the core of an aetiological legend (Coats, 1968:50). However this may be historically, in the present form of the story the naming element plays a minor role and its absence would not affect the action of the narrative in any way.

The problem of the bad water is brought to the attention of Moses by the people. Yet, the people did not come to Moses as the men of Jericho came to Elisha in example 1, asking that the leader, by virtue of his special relationship to Yahweh, would bring supernatural power to bear upon the problem. The people here act more like members of a tour storming up to the tour leader with a complaint about the accommodation. Complaint rather than appeal is the tone. Still, in many other stories of the tradition, Moses is known as one who has access to the powers of Yahweh. Thus, even though the narrative does not indicate that the people were expecting or even demanding a miracle, the problem situation is certainly one to which a miraculous intervention is a possible, even appropriate, response. In fact, miracle was the response to other problem situations in which Moses and the people found themselves in Egypt and in the wilderness. At the very least, here we have a situation which affords an opportunity for a display of Yahweh's power which at the same time would be an act of deliverance for his people.

Moses responds by appealing in turn to Yahweh. It is Yahweh who points out the material to be used but Moses who throws the material into the water. In the first two examples, there were essentially two parties to be considered: the party in trouble and the prophet behind whom stood explicitly or implicitly Yahweh. Here, Yahweh takes an active role with Moses appealing to him for help and following his lead in solving the problem. Can it still be argued that there are only two parties or does Moses have to be seen as a sort of intermediary acting on behalf of both parties? Apart from his crying out to Yahweh, Moses seems to be clearly aligned with the deity. Moses receives the complaint. He throws the wood into the water. Thus, Moses and Yahweh will be taken as the one party corresponding to helper party already noted in the first two examples except that here the action is distributed differently with Yahweh as a more prominent actor. He inititates the response to the people's problem by pointing out the wood, just as Elisha responded in the first example by giving instructions that something be brought. As in the other stories, Moses, as Yahweh's representative, casts the thing brought into the substance causing the trouble. A brief statement reports the result of the action. The water became sweet.

Thus, in spite of a number of differences from the first two examples, this story can be set in an outline resembling the others.

(1) A party discovers a problem. This is brought to the attention of their leader.

(2) The leader appeals to Yahweh. Yahweh responds by indicating to the leader a material with the apparent implication that it be applied to the problem. The leader does this.

(3) The result of the miraculous intervention accompanying the action of the leader is stated.

4. Elisha Recovers an Axe-head Lost in the Jordan (II Kings 6:1-7)

This story is like example 2 in that most of the narrative is devoted to describing the background situation and the details leading up to the crisis. Verses 1 to 5 state the problem and tell how this problem is brought to the attention of the prophet. The composition of this section is worth noting. The members of the prophetic order point out to the prophet that their quarters are too cramped. But in this case neither the action nor the advice of the prophet is requested or expected. The men simply want permission to carry out a proposal, which involves chopping wood at the Jordan. All this simply prepares for the miracle to follow. The prophet is asked by one of the men to come along. Elisha agrees and goes with them. Now the stage is set. The action proceeds as shown in the following summary.

4b. They came to the Jordan and cut wood.

5. When one man was cutting . . . his axe-head fell into the water. He cried out, "I'm in trouble, Master, it was borrowed."

6. The Man of God asked, "Where did it fall?" The man

showed him the place. The Man of God cut a piece of wood
and threw it there. It caused the axe-head to float.
7. The Man of God said, "Pick it up." Then the man reached
    out and got it.

One problem of syntax needs comment. In the last clause of
verse 6, the verb appears to be hiphil and thus apparently
transitive but the total occurrences (once more in the hiphil and
once in the qal) provide a meager basis for discussion. If the verb is
transitive and the "axe-head" is the object, what is the subject? Did
Elisha make the axe-head float or did the stick cause the axe-head
to float? Whether one or the other, the distinction would not seem
to make much difference. Of more importance is the fact that here,
as in example 2, there is no explicit reference to the action of the
deity. The Man of God acts and the miracle occurs. This will be
taken as a matter of emphasis since in this collection of stories
about Elisha and Elijah there is no question that these figures
frequently invoke Yahweh's power quite explicitly. In the
tradition as a whole, they are the kind of persons they are because
of the special relationship they have with Yahweh. Thus, where
the power available to the prophet is not explicitly traced to
Yahweh, this will nevertheless be taken as its source. The party
responding consists of the Man of God with Yahweh in the
background.

The story may be put in the following structural outline similar
to the other examples:

(1) A party falls into a problem situation. The party brings this
    to the attention of the prophet.
(2) The prophet responds with a request for essential
    information which he receives and then takes a material and
    applies it to the problem.
(3) The result is a miraculous occurrence which solves the
    problem.

Only brief comments are required. Verse 7 appears to be
ignored in the above outline. However, the prophet's instruction
to pick up the axe-head followed by the man's compliance does
not add essential information to the story. If verse 7 had been left

out and the story had ended with verse 6, it would be assumed the man somehow got the axe-head back into his possession. Verse 7 is part of the solution to the problem just as the first five verses are part of the statement of the problem. While in most of the preceding examples the first step in the response was an instruction to get a material which was then used to perform the miracle, here the first step in the response is a question asking for more precise information. Material is still used, in this case a stick, but the prophet procures it himself and throws it where it will produce results.

As in the narrative about the poison stew in example 3, the problem situation appears to be a minor crisis compared to other human problems. A number of human solutions are open to the unfortunate workman so that one could see the emphasis in this story more upon the prophet who has the ability to call upon miraculous powers rather than upon the prophet who helps people in genuine need with these powers. Even if this emphasis is granted, the story still has a pattern sufficiently like the others to be classed with them. The need portrayed does not appear to be great, but the power is used to help someone in trouble.

5. Moses Produces Water from the Rock (Exodus 17:1-7)

Comments are needed on a number of points. It was stated earlier that an attempt was going to be made to avoid stories generally supposed to be constructed of more than one source. Here, possible sources are evident to about the same extent as in example 3, which was also from Exodus. According to Coats, there is probably an element of P in verse 1 and, in addition, the explanatory matter in verse 7 could be a deuteronomistic comment (1968:55). However, in the middle section between the last part of verse 1 and the end of verse 6, Noth sees a lack of unity and speaks in his Exodus commentary of doublets. Coats sees complexity but is inclined to trace this to an interweaving of traditions at a preliterary stage. The play on the name Massah in verse 2 is, in his view, a deuteronomistic addition like verse 7. The problems encountered are of the same sort as in example 3, and so it is still possible to use this story.

A broad outline similar to the previous examples can easily be discerned. A problem situation is stated at the beginning: there is no water for the people. This crisis is brought to the attention of Moses and then Yahweh. Yahweh gives instructions that certain things be done and announces that a miracle will happen producing the needed water, when the instructions are carried out. It is stated at the end of the story that this happens.

But there is more to the story than this. The reaction of the people to the lack of water is dealt with in some detail and so this part of the story needs a full discussion. Once the problem of lack of water is stated in verse 1, the people come directly to Moses and ask for water. From the wording used, it would be natural to take the request as a firm demand for rights. Moses does not give any indication that he is going to comply and appeal to Yahweh. He counters with a rhetorical question which indicates that they should not be approaching him in this way with demands. There is a second rhetorical question asking why they are testing Yahweh. It has already been noted that Coats links this second question to verse 7 and traces both to a deuteronomistic tradition, or a group very close to this tradition, in that the whole incident is thus put in a negative light. If this second rhetorical question is left out of consideration, then Moses' response appears to be a simple refusal to do anything for the people.

In verse 3, the people again complain. This time their complaint is not limited to the lack of water. Lack of water is a symptom of a deeper problem; the whole enterprise of leaving Egypt appears to the people to be on the verge of disaster and is characterized as an attempt at mass murder for which Moses is held responsible. This is just one manifestation of the so-called "murmuring motif" which occurs several times (Exodus 14:11, 12; 16:3; Numbers 11:4-6; 14:2, 3; 16:13, 14; 20:3-5, and 21:5). The following elements appear frequently in this motif: the question asking why they were brought into the wilderness, the fear of dying in the wilderness, the wish that they had died, and the charge that Moses had brought them out into the wilderness to kill them. Coats' book is a detailed treatment of this motif.

Moses then appeals to Yahweh to tell him what to do, adding that he is in danger of being killed. Perhaps this last comment is meant to explain why he heeds the people's demand this time while he appeared to reject it the first time.

In some of the miracle stories discussed above, a relatively large amount of space was devoted to the description of the background and events leading up to the problem situation. In this story the problem of lack of water receives very little space, but the means by which the problem situation is brought to the attention of the relevant person is treated in some detail. Nevertheless, this expanded section can be considered a subordinate element of the miracle story because none of the details are resumed at a later point. In other words, the fact that the first demand made to Moses, the murmuring motif, and the apparent threat to Moses' life are reprehensible acts plays no role in the subsequent action of the story in terms of rebuke or punishment by Yahweh. This does not deny these elements any role in the story at all but only argues that in this pattern of action they function as an elaboration of the element seen in all previous examples in which the problem is brought to the attention of the leader or prophet.

Although it is not the aim of this study to look at all kinds of structure, it might be pointed out that, if the whole section, verses 1-7, is taken into account, the possibility of a shift in emphasis is created because a new way of looking at the structure is opened up. The reply of Moses to the people in verse 2, an apparent refusal to do anything for them, is picked up in verse 7 which gives the reason for naming of Massah and Meriba. The miracle story provides the concrete event to which the naming is traced. Verse 7 says, in effect, that the important thing to notice about the miracle story is not the miracle by which Yahweh helped Israel in miraculously providing water but the hostile way in which the demand for water is made. Thus, the explanation in verse 7 uses the miracle story to make a point but this point is contained in the interchange between Moses and the people, which has been identified above as subordinate to the main action. Consequently, if this miracle story is set beside the other examples of miracle stories given above, the usual pattern of Yahweh's response through his representative to help a party in need stands out. Yet, the hostile approach to Moses along with the emphasis of this opens up the possibility of connecting this narrative with other narratives which reflect a pattern of hostility toward Yahweh followed by punishment, a structure which will be considered briefly at a later point. Now, it is true that the full pattern of hostility plus punishment is not present in this story. Still, once the reader or listener is aware of the full pattern from other stories, the mention of the first part of it may then evoke the last part. The hostility brings to mind the possibility of punishment. It is not argued that the whole pattern is thus implicit in this story but only that the possibility of making a connection with the punishment stories is opened up.

Coats has emphasized the tension in this story between the positive and negative evaluation of the people's demand for water, although he does this from the point of view of the history of tradition (1968:59ff.). In his analysis an earlier stage of the tradition sees the incident in a positive light, while a later stage saw the incident in negative terms. Here it will be sufficient to point out that the tension or pull in two different directions emphasized by the comment in verse 7 exists in the miracle story. It is interesting to notice that a miracle story sharing a structure with one set of stories can also reflect a relationship to another set of stories with another structure by virtue of the fact that an element, in this case the bringing of the problem to the attention of the relevant person, is expanded and turned into a hostile exchange between the people and Moses.

In the light of this discussion, the problem situation of the story is in reality more complicated than it appeared at first glance. When Moses finally appeals to Yahweh, he asks that the people be given water on the grounds that his life will be in danger if something is not done. The question might be asked: did Yahweh respond to the people's need for water because of that need or to get his servant Moses out of a bad spot? Perhaps this is a false alternative. At the end of the story it is said that the water came and the people drank indicating that this problem of lack of water is the major one in the story. There is no word at the end to the effect that Moses' life was saved. Consequently, Moses' predicament is a subordinate complication of the problem, solved at the end by implication. For the purpose of making an outline, only the major problem of deficiency of water will be taken into account.

A few further comments are necessary before presenting the outline of this story. As in most of the examples above, the response to the problem begins with instructions. Moses is told to take some of the elders and the staff which he had used earlier to perform miracles. Yahweh also announces what will happen. When Moses strikes the rock, water will come out. Here too an instrument, the staff, is used. The words of Yahweh are not just instructions but also a statement of what will happen perhaps similar in function to the Yahweh word uttered by the prophet in example 1. That Moses followed these instructions and that the miracle occurred are not stated in specific terms but summed up in a brief statement, the last clause of verse 6, in which it is indicated that Moses did this before the eyes of the elders.

The outline of this story, then, can be put down this way:
(1) A party discovers a problem. This is brought to the attention of their leader in a hostile way.
(2) The leader appeals to Yahweh for help with the problem and with the hostility. Yahweh responds by giving instructions which include the use of an instrument and an announcement of a miracle which will remove the problem.
(3) It is stated that the instructions were followed implying that the miracle occurred and the problem was solved.

6. Elijah Brings a Boy Back to Life (I Kings 17:17-24)

Here the problem situation is not connected with some substance like water or stew but with a human being. A boy has died. The crisis is presented very succinctly in verse 17. The boy is the son of a woman known to Elijah. From the present context of the story in chapter 17, she appears to be the woman of the previous story, the widow with whom he was staying. She comes to the prophet to bring her problem to his attention. What she says, however, is not an appeal for his help, at least not directly. She holds him responsible for her calamity. In her view, the presence of the prophet brought her sin to light with the result that punishment struck in the form of the death of her son. It is not clear whether the tone is one of reproach or simply a statement of fact accompanied by the implied suggestion that the prophet go and leave her in peace. Perhaps from the way Elijah phrases his prayer to Yahweh in verse 20 it can be said that the prophet finds the death of the son particularly embarrassing, which suggests that he understood the words of the woman as a reproach. In any event, it is clear that the prophet is acutely aware of his connection with the incident. Furthermore, it is also implied in verse 18 and made clear in verse 20 that without question Yahweh is the one who brought this unfortunate situation about. Now, in the other examples there was little to indicate, even by implication, that Yahweh caused water to go bad or caused the axe-head to be lost or poisoned the stew. To be sure, Moses is held responsible in Exodus 17 for the plight of the people because of his mad scheme to leave Egypt. But this seems to be a different matter. The clamor against Moses can be taken as a kind of rebellion which calls into question his role as leader. The woman's words to the prophet do not explicitly call into question his role as a Man of God but he nevertheless feels that something is at stake here which reflects on his role as a prophet, something which must be dealt with. The crisis can be said to have more than one aspect, as did the crisis in Exodus 17. There is the problem itself, the dead boy, but there is also the effect that the occurrence has on the person closely associated with Yahweh.

The response to the problem is different in a number of ways from the stories considered so far. The response to the problem is rich in detail and several stages are set out in the performance of the miracle. The only instruction given here is the first one, that the women give her son to the prophet. The rest of the verbs in verse 19 describe the actions involved in getting the boy from the mother up to the room on the roof and on to the bed. The next act is the address to Yahweh of verse 20, already mentioned above, in which the responsibility of Yahweh is recognized, and by implication the awkward situation of the prophet in the house of the widow. While in the Moses stories in Exodus 15 and 17 Yahweh speaks or acts when addressed, here he does not become involved by direct action or direct speech, a feature which remains constant in the miracle stories of Elijah and Elisha. Next, there is the physical action of the prophet applied to the boy accompanied by a direct appeal to Yahweh that life be returned. The direct appeal to Yahweh was characteristic of the Moses stories but not of the others. It should be added that this is the first story analyzed in which no material was used as an instrument in the performance of the miracle. Earlier, salt, meal, and wood were thrown on different occasions. A staff was used to strike a rock for water. Here the physical action on the problem involves the prophet's own body when he stretches out on the boy.

The occurrence of the miracle is indicated in verse 22 with the statement that Yahweh heard the prayer and life was restored to the boy. So it is that, even though Yahweh does not act directly in the story, the crucial event of the restoration of life to the boy is clearly seen as Yahweh's response to Elijah's prayer. But the action of the prophet in secluding the boy and stretching out on him three times must also be relevant. Verse 23 simply gives the action of verse 19b in reverse, with the boy being picked up, brought down, and given to his mother. This could be seen simply as a kind of symmetry: the boy is taken away and the boy is brought back. But the story does not end here. The next verse contains a confession by the mother acknowledging that Elijah is a genuine Man of God who speaks the true word of Yahweh. But why this? Was this ever in doubt in the woman's mind? The confession might be related to the woman's reproach to the prophet at the beginning. When this was discussed above, it was left open as to whether a reproach was intended or not. Possibly verse 24 corresponds to verse 18 in that it affirms after the miracle what was called in question before. Consequently, if the problem situation of the story, as suggested above, has two aspects: the death of the boy and the resultant awkward situation created between the prophet and the woman, then the solution of the problem would have to resolve both these matters by bringing the boy back to life and by re-instating the prophet in the woman's eyes. It might even be argued that the most important element in the problem, thus understood, was the status of the prophet, and that the death of the boy was just the occasion upon which this was called into question. This interpretation need not be pressed here. It is not necessary to define all aspects of the problem in order to be able to outline the story at a sufficiently generalized level to compare it with the others. Still, it is worth mentioning especially since in the previous example the problem situation had more than one aspect: the need of the people and the difficult position of Moses who was held responsible. In this Elijah story, the problem situation is expanded in much the same direction. It is not only a question of the need of the woman who has lost her son but also the embarrassing situation of the prophet.

The story of I Kings 17:17-24 can be outlined as follows:
(1) The party discovers a problem. This is brought to the attention of the prophet.
(2) The prophet responds by taking the boy, acting on him and offering prayer that he be restored.
(3) The boy is restored to life and to his mother.

The parallel account in II Kings 4:18-37 has been discussed above in Part II. There is no need to repeat anything here. The only important difference was in the fact that the same framework was simply filled out with much more detail. The comparison of the two stories showed clearly how the same story can be told in a longer and a shorter form. The material present only in the longer version is subordinate to the main structure shared by the two stories, and so could be omitted from the longer story without seriously distorting the structure. The structural outline given in

Part II was the structure common to these two stories. It was stated so specifically that it could only be used for these two stories. In order to show the common structure which these two stories share with other miracle stories, it is necessary to generalize the outline and make it more abstract. This illustrates very well how one may select different levels of abstraction depending on material being compared and the reason for comparing.

7. Elisha Helps a Widow Who Is in Debt (II Kings 4:1-7)

This story begins like example 1. The problem is not described separately and then followed by an appeal to the prophet, but the appeal itself reveals the nature of the trouble. The problem situation here is different from all the others described so far. The problem cannot be located in a substance or a material or a human being but lies in a threatened event. A creditor is about to take the widow's two sons as slaves. The initial response of the prophet is not as in most other cases instructions but a question. He demands information about what is in the house so that he will know how to proceed further. In one other instance, example 4, the response also began with a question. This was when the prophet asked where the axe-head had fallen. Here, when the prophet learns that only a jug of oil is left, he gives a series of instructions. The woman and her sons follow these instructions and discover that a miracle has happened, providing a great quantity of oil. Giving these instructions is the only action of the prophet in the situation. Contrary to previous examples, he is not present when the miracle occurs. Yet the miracle does happen. However, the story cannot end here because the problem is not solved. The step from the miracle to the solution of the problem is provided for by another instruction from the prophet to sell the oil in order to provide money to pay off the debt. The story stops without any description of the woman obeying this instruction. There is no need to hear more, since it is now known how the miracle can lead to the solution of the problem of the debt. Thus, this last instruction from the prophet functions as an explanation of how the problem was solved, whereas the preceding instruction prepared the way for the occurrence of the miracle.

Even though there are significant differences between this story and those discussed in examples 1 to 6, the outline is similar enough to warrant presenting it with the others.

(1) A party brings its problem situation to the attention of the prophet.

(2) The prophet responds with a request for essential information and then he gives instructions which when carried out are accompanied by a miracle.

(3) Further instructions indicate how the results of the miracle may be used to solve the problem.

Summary of Examples 1 to 7

Each of the foregoing examples was given an outline or generalized statement of the pattern of action. While all seven outlines represent roughly the same degree of generalization, these outlines are not identical. Is it possible by generalizing further to state a single outline of the action which these stories could be said to share as a group? If the clues mentioned earlier are followed with special attention paid to basic roles and actions seen in terms of function, then one might say that there are two basic roles, the party in need and the party able to help, and two basic actions, the appeal for help and the response giving miraculous help. In addition, the problem creating the need for help and the solving of this problem are stated or implied. It should be clear, and it is worth emphasizing again, that outlines are not looked upon as absolute but relative. A given outline holds true for a given set of stories. The form the outline takes in the number and kind of elements and the degree of abstraction or generalization to which each of the elements is taken depends upon the number of stories being considered and the extent to which they vary in detail. The aim at this stage is not to make outlines which would have absolute validity but to make outlines which might prove useful in drawing attention to and defining more precisely the nature of structures in the biblical text which show similarity to each other.

The seven stories can be presented in a chart. In the chart the stories have been divided into three main elements which can be set down briefly here.

Chart of Examples 1 to 7

(1) Problem - A brings to attention of B

Example 1	bad water	men of Jericho tell Elisha
Example 2	poison stew	brotherhood tells Elisha
Example 3	bitter water	people complain to Moses
		Moses appeals to Yahweh
Example 4	axe-head in water	man tells Elisha
Example 5	no water	people complain to Moses
		Moses appeals to Yahweh
Example 6	death of boy	woman tells Elijah (reproaches?)
Example 7	threat of debt	widow appeals to Elisha

(2) Responds

		material	action	
1.	Elijah instructs get material	salt	throws	word of Yahweh
2.	Elisha instructs get material	meal	throws	
3.	Yahweh shows Moses material	stick	throws	
4.	Elisha questions	stick	throws	
5.	Yahweh instructs Moses	staff	hits rock	Yahweh announces water will come
6.	Elijah instructs get boy		stretches on boy prays to heal	
7.	Elisha questions		instructs what to do	

(3) Miraculous result reported	Problem solved
1. water restored	
2. Elisha instructs pour out stew	nothing bad in pot
3. water sweet	
4. axe-head floats	
5. Moses did as instructed by Yahweh	
6. boy restored to life	Elijah gives boy back to mother confession of mother
7. oil flows into vessels	Elisha instructs to sell

In the chart, the stories have been divided into three main elements which can be set down briefly here.

(1) A party in a problem situation brings this to the attention of a party with power to provide miraculous help.

(2) The helper party responds by taking action on the problem.

(3) The miraculous result which removes the problem is indicated.

The first element contains the depiction of a party (person or persons) in a problem situation who brings this to the attention of a party known to provide miraculous help (a prophet or Moses with a varying degree of participation by Yahweh). It might be argued that the first element could be divided into two: a delineation of a problem situation *and* the bringing of this to the attention of a prophet or a leader. This is conceded. However, in two instances (examples 1 and 7) the problem is stated in an appeal to the prophet. Then, too, from the point of view of the miracle story a problem situation is not important in itself except as it involves a person or persons who usually come expecting a response from the leader. Moreover, the action in the story does not really start with the existence of a problem situation which may have existed for a long time, but with this problem coming to the attention of a person who is able to act on it. It must be admitted, however, that when the parties bring problems to the attention of the leader it is not always clear what kind of response they expect. There is not always a statement clearly phrased as an appeal. What is said can be understood as complaint or even reproach. But even though the words of the party bringing the problem to the attention of the prophet or leader may not clearly indicate an appeal for help, it is plain from the structure of the story that this represents an occasion for a miracle.

The second element contains the response of the party to the attention of whom the problem is brought. The role of this party who is made aware of the problem situation and who acts on it with a miracle should probably be considered a shared role because Yahweh always participates in this response, even if the only indication of his presence is the fact that a miracle has occurred. And so the role of one who responds is assumed in varying proportions by Yahweh and by his representative, if Elijah, Elisha, and Moses can be described by this word for the purposes of the discussion of these stories. To be sure, as already indicated, it is assumed that the context of these stories in biblical tradition implies that any supernatural or miraculous power must be ultimately traced to Yahweh. In some cases, such as examples 3 and 5, Yahweh participates by receiving the complaint through Moses and indicating what Moses should do to have the needed miracle performed. In the chart more details of each response have been given than are in fact necessary. The specific elements of response are by no means present in all examples. For instance, an instruction to get something which will be used in performing the miracle stands at the beginning of the response in examples 1 and 2. A similar indication to employ something in solving the problems stands at the beginning of the response in example 3. Instructions are also at the beginning of the response in 5 and 6. Then again, a material (salt, meal, sticks) is thrown by the representative in the first four examples. An instrument is used in the fifth example. There is no instrument in example 6 and the prophet is not even present in example 7. It could even be argued that the first four examples fit into a group because in each case material is thrown. These details are worth noting and were thus included in the chart. However, the decision was made to describe the response only in general terms, saying that the representative took action, on his own or on instructions from Yahweh, on the problem which would cover examples 1 to 6 but would also include the last example in which the prophet issues instructions to be carried out in his absence.

The third element is the assertion or indication that a miraculous event has taken place. A great deal of discussion and argument could flow from the use of the term "miracle" but all that is meant is that something occurs which is not expected under normal circumstances and which appears traceable to the intervention of Yahweh. Normally, the narrative simply states briefly what has occurred. There are in some cases instructions accompanying this statement but they are ones logically connected with the occurrence of the miracle. The instruction is given to pour out the stew. The man is told to pick up the axe-head floating on the water. The widow is told to sell the oil.

Two Examples of a Different Type

Not all stories involving a miracle can be grouped with the seven examples just given. To illustrate this point two stories will be set out briefly here. The structure which they have in common is different from that of the preceding examples.

8. The Man of God Increases Food (II Kings 4:42-44)

Although the name Elisha is not used in the story, its context among other stories links it with Elisha. There is no problem to which the miracle is a response. A man brings twenty loaves of bread to the Man of God and some other food. What this other food was, if in fact the reference is to food, is in doubt because of the difficulty of the last two words of 42a (Gray, 1970:501f; Montgomery, 1951:373). Following the background material of verse 42a, the action of the narrative begins. The Man of God gives an instruction to distribute the food to the people so that they may eat. The objection is raised that this small amount will not go far before a hundred men. Now, this is a problem of sorts but not like those in earlier examples. Here, there is no mention of lack of food. The only problem is one created by the prophet when he instructs that something be done which is not possible by human standards. The prophet has taken the initiative by giving an instruction. He is not responding to a problem brought to his attention. The objection raised prepares the way for the miracle to follow by drawing attention to the difficulty posed by the instruction as seen from the human viewpoint. The reply of the prophet to the objection is twofold. First, he repeats word for word the instruction he just gave. Then he adds a subordinate explanatory clause containing a word of Yahweh which indicates that there will be enough and some left over. The last verse of this short narrative shows that the instruction was obeyed. The people ate and had something to spare, with the added note that this was according to the Yahweh word which the Man of God had spoken.

(1) Background elements are stated which set a scene necessary for the action.

(2) The prophet gives an instruction.

(3) The person instructed objects that the instruction is not possible.

(4) The prophet gives the same instruction again adding a word of Yahweh indicating that what is instructed will be made possible.

(5) It is stated that the instruction is obeyed and it happens as the word of Yahweh said.

9. Elijah Increases the Widow's Supply of Meal and Oil (I Kings 17:8-16)

For the moment, verse 8 will be taken as the beginning of the story. Since this story is being set beside the previous example, the ways in which it is similar to this example will be of first importance. A word of Yahweh instructs Elijah to go to Zarephath to live where a widow will provide food for him. He obeys without argument or hesitation. When he finds a woman gathering sticks, he instructs her to get him some water to drink. She does so without objection but, when he instructs her to bring him some bread, she points out to the prophet that she has only enough food for one last meal for her son and herself. They plan to eat this and then die. In effect, this reply to the instruction indicates the impossibility of obeying. The prophet's response to this is twofold: he repeats his instruction, although not in exactly the same words, insisting that his cake be made first; then comes a subordinate explanatory clause containing a word of Yahweh announcing that the meal and oil will not lack until rain comes. The reference to rain and indeed the whole situation of the story indicates a famine, a situation existing in the incidents preceding and following this segment, but more of this later. Verses 15 and 16 indicate that the instructions were obeyed and that the meal and oil lasted, closing with the statement that this was according to the Yahweh word spoken through Elijah.

The similarities between this story and the previous one are striking at many points. The outline given for example 8 can be used for this story without change. In this story, longer than the other, two instructions are given: (1) to get water, which was immediately obeyed without question and (2) to get food, the story discussed above. The first instruction in verses 10b and 11a does not seem to be an indispensable part of the action. From the point of view of the structural outline used here, it is a subordinate structure. Perhaps it should be taken as part of the element numbered (2), since an instruction obeyed without objection presents a good contrast to the following instruction which evokes a protest from the woman.

On the other hand, this story does depict a genuine case of human need. A widow and her son are on the verge of starving to death. It might then be possible to class this story with examples 1 to 7 since the structure of this story can be set in an outline very much like the common pattern of these first seven examples. If this were done, verses 8 to 12 could be taken as the statement of a problem. The crisis comes to the prophet's attention through his instructions to the woman to get him bread to eat because she then must explain why she cannot do what he has asked. Verses 13 and 14 would be response of the prophet to the need of the woman. He tells he what to do and adds a word of Yahweh announcing the miraculous happening which will solve her problem. It must be admitted that the three elements of the outline attributed to the first seven examples (the problem brought to the attention of the prophet, the response of the prophet, the occurrence of the miracle) are present in this story.

However, of the two possible ways of describing the structure of this story, the link with example 8 seems to be the stronger. Even so, this does not mean that the second possibility is to be rejected. The three-element pattern attributed here to examples 1 to 7 is still to be discerned behind the more dominant five-element pattern described above in example 8. The possibility of seeing two patterns simply means that the narrative has two facets. The larger one reflects a similarity to the story of example 8, while the smaller one reflects a similarity to the structure shared by the stories of examples 1 to 7. Here the story is classed with example 8 because the affinity between the two seems to be stronger.

Finally, the problem of defining the limits of this story must be mentioned. It was suggested above that the selection of verse 8 as the beginning of this story was a decision taken only for the purposes of the initial discussion. Verse 7 refers to the drying up of a wadi, which plays a role in the preceding verses, a place to which Elijah had been sent by a word of Yahweh. Yet the drying up of the wadi will leave him without water, and so this occurrence provides the ground for another word of Yahweh. In fact, the whole first part of the chapter hangs together rather nicely in a framework. Verses 1 to 16 may be summarized as follows:

1. Elijah announces a drought to Ahab.
2. A word of Yahweh comes to him: "Go . . . hide in the Wadi Cherith . . . I will see to it that the ravens feed you there."
5. He went and it happened this way
7. . . . the wadi dries up . . .
8. A word of Yahweh comes to him: ". . . go to Zarephath . . . and live there . . . I will see to it that a widow will feed you."
10-16. He goes and it happens this way.

In other words, the miracle story examined as example 9 has been integrated into the structure just summarized above. The drought is announced and comes but it appears that Yahweh is going to take care of his prophet. Two sections having the same structure depict Yahweh's care for his prophet. Each section begins with identical wording (verses 2 and 8). A word of Yahweh comes to Elijah containing an instruction to go to a certain place and an announcement that Yahweh will ensure that he will be looked after. This is followed by the description of how Elijah follows the instructions and how the promise of Yahweh that he will be cared for comes true. In the first instance the element describing how he is cared for is found in one verse, verse 5. But in the second instance this element takes up the section from verse 10 to verse 16, which may indicate the true boundaries of the miracle story. In other words, the miracle story (verses 10 to 16) is part of and functions within a larger structure. Here it is the last element explaining how the promise of Yahweh came true.

Five Examples Where Intervention Comes as Punishment

To complement the nine miracle stores already dealt with, five stories will be analyzed in which a punishment involving a supernatural intervention is a central point of the story. As with the other examples, short narratives will be selected and those usually thought to be composed of more than one literary source will be avoided.

10. Elisha Curses the Boys (II Kings 2:23-25)

The prophet is on his way to Bethel and some small boys make fun of him. Measured by the outcome of the story, this is a serious offense. Since this act of irreverence or impiety was directed toward the prophet, he responds by cursing the boys in the name of Yahweh. Verse 42b describes how the curse once uttered becomes a reality as bears come out of the forest and lacerate forty-two boys.

The story may be outlined as follows:

(1) A group commits a wrong action against the prophet.

(2) The prophet curses this group in the name of Yahweh.

(3) A misfortune befalls the group, and this appears to be the result of the curse.

11. Yahweh Sends Fire on the People (Numbers 11:1-3)

This story is brief but different and more complex than example 10. In the first party of the story there is no human figure, leader, or prophet, to share Yahweh's role. The people appear to be complaining. Although the content of the complaint is not given, it clearly reflects badly on Yahweh since he becomes angry and burns the people with his fire which destroys the edges of the camp. Since the story is so short we are left to imagine a great deal. What damage was done up to this point? Were people actually being killed or was the fire at the edge of the camp only a threat poised to destroy the camp? At the very least this direct intervention by Yahweh posed a serious threat.

Up to this point the story is similar to example 10 in two major ways at least. First one party, here the people, behaves wrongly toward another party, Yahweh. Second, the response is punishment. In this case, however, there is no pronouncement which would give warning that a punishment was coming as the cursing preceded the punishment in the previous story. Still, in the first story it can be taken that the prophet is playing a representative role. He curses the boys in the name of Yahweh, showing that the power comes in the name of Yahweh and also that the act of impiety was judged to be ultimately against Yahweh. In the Elisha story, a role is shared between Yahweh and the prophet, with the prophet filling the role almost completely. In this story from Numbers, there is no representative and the role is in no way shared.

But the story is not finished. The punishment through fire, whether existing only as a threat or having actually begun, is stopped through the action of Moses. Thoroughly terrified, the people appeal to Moses who then prays to Yahweh. This action has its effect. The fire subsides. But what role is Moses playing here? To the extent that he is acting on behalf of the people he would seem to be aligned more with them than with Yahweh as far as roles are concerned. Yet the fact that his prayer is answered right away makes clear that he stands in a special relationship to Yahweh. The people know this and also know that their prayers would hardly have the same effect. Moses has been granted by Yahweh a special status by virtue of which his intercessions have more weight than those of the people. It is interesting to note, as has been pointed out, that in the first part of this story no such person is mentioned.

Thus an outline of this story might run this way:
(1) The people commit a wrong against Yahweh.
(2) Yahweh becomes angry and undertakes a punishment against the people.
(3) The people appeal to Moses who prays to Yahweh.
(4) The punishment undertaken by Yahweh stops.

The people do wrong and the punishment follows but does not take its full effect. The last part of this outline bears some similarity to the problem stories of examples 1 to 7 while the first part of the outline is similar to the story of example 11. The punishment from Yahweh is, as far as the reaction of the people goes, treated much like a problem such as a shortage of water or food. They appeal to Moses, the usual person to call on in such emergencies. He does what he did in the problem stories. He passes on the concern of the people to Yahweh. The critical difference in all this is the fact that the danger facing the people is not some natural danger, one of the hazards of human existence, but the anger of Yahweh materialized in such a way as to threaten their destruction. In a sense this story is a blend of the kind of punishment story seen in example 10 and the kind of story discussed in examples 1 to 7.

12. Yahweh Punishes the People with Serpents (Numbers 21:4-9)

Apart from verse 4a there is little in this section to indicate literary sources (Coats, 1968:116). The present story follows the pattern of the preceding example fairly closely. The people in the wilderness take up their complaint against Yahweh and Moses in a version of the so-called murmuring motif. They do not like the food and water situation, but this specific complaint serves as a starting point for attacking the departure from Egypt with the argument that the adventure will end with the death of everyone. In other stories containing a complaint about food and water, such as in example 5 above, the problem of lack of water was met with a miracle which eliminated the need. The complaint was ignored. Here, the matter of complaint is central and taken as a serious wrong against Yahweh. The immediate response is punishment by serpents which bite the people so that a great number of them die. The people appeal to Moses, asking him to pray to Yahweh so that he will remove the punishment which is killing them off. At the same time, the people admit that they have sinned in speaking against Yahweh and Moses. The interest of the story then shifts from the attack of the serpents viewed as a punishment to the attack viewed as a problem which the people must appeal to Yahweh to have removed. Moses prays on behalf of the people. Yahweh responds by giving Moses instructions to make a serpent and put it on a standard. These instructions are followed by an announcement that if anyone who is bitten looks at the serpent he will survive. The last verse of the narrative, verse 9, simply states that Moses followed instructions and all who looked at the serpent survived.

The following outline can be drawn up:

(1) The people commit a wrong against Yahweh.
(2) Yahweh undertakes a punishment against the people.
(3) The people appeal to Moses who prays to Yahweh.
(4) Yahweh responds with instructions to Moses accompanied by an announcement that those who perform a certain act will recover.
(5) Moses follows instructions and it is reported that persons who perform the act recover as Yahweh announced.

Here again, the structure is a blend of a kind of punishment story and a story of Yahweh's miraculous help. The result of the punishment, people dying off from an attack of serpents, becomes the situation of need out of which the people appeal to Yahweh through Moses for help. Instructions are given to make something which then becomes instrumental in numerous miraculous healings. This story has been outlined in five elements while the preceding story has only four elements. The reason for this is that in example 11 the prayer of Moses is answered directly so that the fire subsides. This story, however, runs much more like example 1 to 7 in that the response to the appeal is more complicated. Instructions are issued which have to be carried out and an announcement is made of the miracle to happen which must then be seen to come true.

13. Miriam and Aaron Oppose Moses (Numbers 12:1-16)

In this chapter it seems fairly certain that different literary sources do not play a role. However, there are apparent tensions and marks of unevenness which have led some to suggest that two traditions have been combined; but it is not possible to untangle the present text to reveal two separate accounts. As mentioned earlier, stories with complications have been avoided in order to provide good examples for an initial discussion of the kind of analysis practiced in this present study. Even though this story appears to be more complicated than previous examples, it may still prove a useful example.

In verses 1 and 2a, Miriam and Aaron are speaking against Moses. But, with regard to the two issues raised, how is the issue of the Cushite woman (whatever that is precisely) related to their challenge of Moses' position as the unique channel of Yahweh's communication? The second of the two charges is at least clearly stated and followed up in the rest of the narrative, so it can be said that the wrong done here is mainly the challenge of Moses' role as sole spokesman for Yahweh, whatever other dimensions the opposition may be assumed to have.

At the end of verse 2 it is noted that Yahweh heard. Verse 4 gives his initial response, which is to invite the three to the tent where he comes down in a pillar of cloud. In a speech to Aaron and Miriam,

Yahweh rejects their charge against Moses and affirms his special status. The speech ends with a question asking why they were not afraid to speak against Moses. All this amounts to an authoritative declaration of the fact that Miriam and Aaron were wrong. As the speech of Yahweh comes to an end, it is then reported that his anger burned. After Yahweh has left, it is discovered that Miriam's skin has become diseased and is white as snow, a punishment administered by Yahweh for the wrong committed. Of course, we are left to ask why only Miriam was struck and to this question many answers might be given. However, in verse 11, when Aaron appeals to Moses, he associates himself with Miriam by saying that they had both sinned. Consequently, in spite of unanswered questions, a certain continuity is preserved in the narrative.

As in the two previous narratives, the physical manifestation of the punishment is the occasion of an appeal to Moses. Here, it is Aaron who appeals on behalf of Miriam (verses 11 and 12). In the next verse, Moses appeals to Yahweh to heal Miriam. Yahweh's answer indicates that this will happen only after a period outside the camp. Miriam's healing is not reported but, since she spent the required time outside the camp, the restoration of health can be assumed.

If the foregoing description is acceptable as a sketch of the main features of the narrative, the following outline can be set out to show the similarities this story has with examples 11 and 12 above.

(1) The two commit a wrong against Yahweh.
(2) He declares them in the wrong and inflicts a punishment.
(3) Aaron appeals to Moses who prays to Yahweh.
(4) Yahweh responds with a stipulation implying that if that is carried out the disease will be healed.
(5) It is reported that the stipulation is carried out and it can be assumed that the miracle took place.

Two further comments can be made. First of all, the wrong was against Moses but the issue was his special status with Yahweh and so the element numbered (1) states that the wrong is against

Yahweh. Secondly, Yahweh declares in some detail how and why the pair are wrong. The speech is rather lengthy for this short narrative. Since the speech is rather important for the assessment of the figure of Moses in the tradition as a whole, it might be argued that the information given here about the role of Moses is more important than the punishment of Miriam which lasted only briefly anyway. But perhaps this illustrates again what has been suggested before, namely, that different aspects of stories stand out depending on what other material they are set beside. When this story is set beside the two preceding examples, the similarities described in outline appear prominent.

14. Cain Kills Abel (Genesis 4:1-16)

It may seem strange to include this well-known story in a list of "miracle stories" but it was explained earlier that this label was chosen for its convenience rather than its accuracy. The punishment laid on Cain in the form of a curse is miraculous according to the way in which the term was defined above. Yahweh intervenes through the curse to force a change in the kind of life open to Cain. But whether or not this story can be called a miracle story, even according to the loose definition suggested, is not of prime importance. The important point is to establish whether or not this story shows up sufficient structural similarities when set beside the other punishment stories considered above.

An outline consisting of wrong, punishment, appeal, and mitigation like that in the three preceding stories can be found. Cain murders his brother (verse 8). Yahweh questions him about his brother, in much the same way as he had questioned Adam and Eve after they had eaten the forbidden fruit. Then, after Yahweh indicates that he knows about the crime, he announces his punishment as a curse, again with some similarity to the pronouncements in Genesis 3. Cain replies to Yahweh that the punishment is too much for him and that, left to wander unprotected, he would soon meet his end. Now, this is not phrased like an appeal and so could be taken in several ways. It could be taken as a complaint about the severity of the sentence. Or, it could be read as a simple statement of fact. It could be taken as an indirect appeal, since the statement of the implications of the sentence is a way of appealing for leniency. Yet, in examples 3 and 5 above the reaction of the people to the problem facing them could be taken as demand or complaint. Even this way of bringing their problem to the attention of Yahweh was met with a positive response from him. Similarly, whether the tone of Cain's words is appeal or complaint, he draws Yahweh's attention to his precarious situation with the result that Yahweh takes action to see that Cain will not lose his life in the way he has feared. Strictly speaking, this act of kindness from Yahweh may not be mitigation of the punishment. The original terms still stand. Yet a side effect, apparently overlooked by Yahweh, is countered so that the limits of the punishment are clearly marked. The story ends on a positive rather than a negative note.

There is still the material in verses 1 to 7 which needs explanation. If the story as a whole can be looked upon as a punishment story which nevertheless ends on a positive note, the material of these opening verses can be viewed as a subordinate section which sets the stage for Cain's action. Even if this section may be considered subordinate from the point of view of the punishment structure, the contents are striking and present important material. The crime of Cain is fratricide. But, more than this, the murder is the result of a rivalry not just between two brothers but between two kinds of people, the shepherds and the farmers. For a reason not given in the story, Yahweh has looked with favor upon Abel's offering but not upon Cain's. It was Cain's anger in response to this that led to the death of Abel. The notoriously difficult speech of Yahweh in verse 7 seems to be some sort of warning about Cain's anger. Since this opening section is so loaded with material, one would have to ask whether the real interest of the story does not lie here, so that the following punishment of Cain is almost secondary. That is to say, does the grand image of two rival ways of life, shepherding and farming, with Yahweh's favor of one leading to fratricide dominate? It has been argued above on more than one occasion that we must be open to the possibility of a great richness and complexity in stories. Since there are other stories in Genesis 1-11 which contain a punishment element, the punishment structure described above seems to stand out in the present setting (Westermann, 1964:51ff.). In this view, the first seven verses would then be background and thus a story within a story, being a developed description of the wrong done.

The similarity in the narrative pattern of this story to the outlines of examples 11, 12, and 13 are significant enough to make worthwhile including this story here. The punishment section also stands close to example 10. Nevertheless, differences cannot be glossed over. In the first place, there are only two characters involved in the punishment structure, Yahweh and Cain. There is no leader or prophet figure involved in the punishment or Yahweh's kindness to Cain afterwards. Perhaps since Cain is a second generation human, this stands to reason. But, even in the three previous examples, the first part of the story did not involve Moses. Then again, it was seen here that the last part of the story does not contain a clear appeal. Nor is the response of Yahweh to Cain's remark clearly a mitigation of the punishment. Consequently, the differences should lead to a certain amount of caution about this example.

The story can be outlined in the following way:
(1) Cain does wrong against Yahweh.
(2) Yahweh makes clear to him that he has done wrong and announces his punishment.
(3) Cain points out what the consequence of such a judgment will be for him.
(4) Yahweh acts to prevent such a consequence.
(5) It is reported that Cain leaves to live out his punishment.

Comments on Examples 10 Through 14

The patterns of these stories are not all alike, and so there does not seem to be any advantage in trying to state a common or shared outline for all five. Example 10 is different from the others in two ways. There is no mitigation of the punishment and Elisha is involved in mediating the miraculous punishment. Nevertheless, this story is valuable because it is an example of a short punishment story without the added mitigation stage. The last story, example 14, is so close to examples 11 to 13 that it is worth including in this study, yet because of the differences already discussed it will not be set with the others but given the status of a very good possibility.

Examples 11 through 13 could be called complex in that the first part of the narrative is similar in structure to example 10 and the last part of the narrative is similar to examples 1 to 7. The interesting thing about the punishment segments of these narratives is that the structure is even simpler than that of example 10. In this story there are the three steps outlined: wrong done to the prophet, pronouncement of a curse by the prophet on the wrongdoers, and the realization of the curse in the punishment of the wrongdoers. But in the three complex stories the punishment section has only two steps: the party does wrong and Yahweh brings down punishment. There is no announcement of a punishment followed by the description of the occurrence of the punishment. The difference is the presence of a prophet or some other figure. Since such a person is a kind of mediator of Yahweh's power, then there is less likely to be the direct kind of action in bringing on the punishment than when Yahweh alone is concerned and acts without any human figure like a prophet or Moses.

The three stories listed as examples 11 through 13 can be said to have the following outline in common:
(1) A party commits a wrong against Yahweh.
(2) Yahweh responds with a miraculous punishment.
(3) The party appeals to Yahweh's representative who prays to Yahweh.
(4) Yahweh responds by mitigating the punishment.
It should be noted that the element numbered (4) is rather different in each case. In example 11, the response is simply that the fire stops. In example 12, instructions are given to Moses to

make something and use it to counteract the problem. This is done and the problem is counteracted. In example 13, it is indicated by Yahweh that a small penalty must be paid after which the original punishment will be lifted. Nevertheless, in all three stories this element functions in the same way by relating that the punishment was mitigated. Again it should be emphasized that the outline just given as the outline common to all three stories is not an absolute outline for a punishment-mitigation form but a relative outline. It is valid for these three stories. If a wide range of stories were being brought together, it might be considered useful to state the common or shared outline differently, or to group the stories into sets and use more than one outline.

It was suggested earlier that these three stories could be considered complex in that there are two points where Yahweh intervenes in each one: the punishment and the mitigation. These stories should be set beside the first nine miracle stories because they reflect a pattern which shows that Yahweh not only intervened to help people afflicted with various natural disasters and troubles but also those who were clearly the recipients of his punishment.

CONCLUDING COMMENTS

Now that the biblical material has been reviewed, an attempt may be made to summarize and evaluate what has been done. In all, fourteen stories have been considered. The first nine involved divine intervention for the purpose of helping, or intervention in a positive sense; the last five involved negative intervention, that is, for the purpose of punishment, although in the last four of these there is a further intervention of a positive sort to mitigate the punishment. It was seen that examples 1 to 7 could be grouped together. A common or shared outline with three steps was proposed which showed a movement through three phases: problem, response, and problem solved. Further, examples 11 through 13 could be grouped together with a common outline of four phases: wrong, punishment, appeal, mitigation. These stories were called complex because they seemed to consist of two patterns which were found alone elsewhere.

Even though the review of these narratives was characterized earlier as more of an exploration than a systematic analysis, a serious attempt was made to carry out an orderly, controlled description. As already indicated, the use of a group of similar stories, some of which are very short, was the main device employed to guide the description of structure. The very short stories provided minimal frameworks and thus excellent starting points from which to attack other longer and more complicated stories. The use of a group of similar narratives provided a means of comparison so that the individual narratives exercised a mutual control on each other in determining the common pattern and also the degree of abstraction in which it should be stated. Thus, the pattern or structure found was said to be relative to the group being compared. Throughout this procedure, attention was focused primarily on main actors and actions, seeking in the process of comparison to state these in terms of the roles of actors and the function of actions in the plot. All of this analysis involved restatement of the narratives in a condensed but generalized form. With the shortest stories, this meant relatively little change. With longer narratives, lengthy sections had to be subsumed under brief headings. Initially, with the shorter stories, a rule of thumb was introduced to assist in the reduction to frameworks in that a tentative distinction was made between essential and non-essential parts of the narrative. The non-essential parts were basically what could be left out and still leave a story. It is certainly true that there is a good measure of vagueness and lack of precision surrounding all these manoevres. In the end, one must simply ask the question: are the results of the analysis sufficiently interesting to justify playing it by ear for the time being on the side of method? These answer given here is yes.

A few further comments can be made about actors and actions. In sorting out the main actors into roles, it was argued that the role of the one who responded to the need was filled by a party of two, Yahweh and his representative. It was found convenient to do this in spite of manifest problems. For example, Yahweh was present only in some narratives by implication in that his power ultimately lay behind the miracle, while in the Moses stories he participated equally with his representative. Who fills the role of helper or how the role is shared may turn out later to be important distinctions to develop. At this stage, however, it seems more useful to suppress these distinctions in favor of seeing clearly the general movement in the seven miracle stories which were grouped together.

Similarly, many different kinds of actions were lumped together in the generalizing process. For example, the actions which functioned as a response to the need were quite varied. Throwing something was the most common but there was also hitting, stretching, praying, and giving instructions (see chart of examples 1 to 7). On two occasions, a pronouncement of Yahweh was also involved. As with the question of actors and roles, these distinctions are not without importance and will bear further investigation.

In developing this particular way of looking at stories, several choices were made. Since narratives are incredibly complex items of language with many aspects and levels, most scholars who seek to describe narrative structure are selective, focusing on a limited number of these according to what they feel is important or relevant. In the above discussion of miracle stories, neither grammatical nor stylistic markers played a role since the patterns described are above these two levels of discourse. In correlating stories of different length and different content, grammatical and stylistic markers were not of immediate help. Nor has use been made of the analytical devices such as the codes and grids frequently employed in current structural analysis, although a general familiarity with this kind of research has had its influence. Nevertheless, what has been attempted shares with these others the concentration on texts and the linguistic and literary patterns which make texts what they are.

At this point, it might be added that this approach to the miracle stories strikes texts at a different level than is usual in form critical and tradition historical studies where the concern is with form and function, that is, patterns in the text influenced by the setting in which the text lived. In his commentary on Exodus, Brevard Childs has identified two patterns which "can be detected in the structure of the stories which contain the murmuring theme" (1974:258). Pattern I (initial need, complaint, intercession, miraculous intervention) can be seen in Exodus 15:22f. and 17:1ff. as well as in Numbers 20:1-13. Pattern II (complaint, anger and punishment, intercession, reprieve) is found in Numbers 11:1-3, 17:6-15, and 21:4-10. According to Childs, these patterns go back to a period of oral tradition and must have had some function at this stage. While he can imagine that each pattern originally served a separate function, he claims that both, even at the oral stage, soon came to have the same function in that these stories "lent themselves to a homiletical purpose and served as a warning against resistance to God's plan for the nation" (259). It will be noticed that Pattern I is roughly the pattern identified behind examples 1 to 7 and that the two stories from Exodus mentioned by Childs are examples 3 and 5 in the seven. Pattern II is roughly the pattern identified behind examples 10 through 13 and two of the examples mentioned by Childs are numbers 11 and 12 of that group. However, Childs views his two patterns as stories containing the murmuring theme. Starting from this very specific literary context, he seeks to move back into the oral period in order to suggest how these patterns may have functioned. In what was done above, the patterns were seen in a broader range of stories with rather different content. Thus, the patterns were stated more abstractly and no attempt was made to move back to settings.

Similarly, one may turn to the work of Burke Long on the stories of the prophets (1973a, 1973b) where some of the stories treated in this part are mentioned. Approaching the question of genre through form and function, Long identifies an "oracle-actualization narrative" (1973a:346f.). To this category, he would assign example 1 (II Kings 2:19-22), example 8 (II Kings 4:42-44), and example 9 (I Kings 17:8-16) because they contain a divine oracle and have a common pattern (situation/crisis; divine oracle; fulfillment/resolution of crisis). Long argues that these stories must be kept separate from stories like example 2 (II Kings 4:38-41), example 4 (II Kings 6:1-7), example 7 (II Kings 4:1-7), and example 10 (II Kings 2:23-25) in which the aim is to "venerate the holy man and his exclusive, awe-inspiring powers" (1973a:346). The decision was made above not to set apart stories with an oracle or Yahweh word from the others as a special case. Thus, examples 1 to 7 were grouped together and examples 8 and 9 were offered as examples of narratives departing from the pattern seen in the first seven. In other words, it may be relevant to make such a distinction at the form critical level but it was not considered useful to do it in the study presented here. As Long's study shows, form critics are interested in patterns very similar to those discussed here, but they work with a more specific statement of patterns since the link with setting is important. The patterns discussed above were examined as repeated patterns in a body of literature, the Hebrew Bible, and not from the point of view of origin and function in a life situation (Culley, 1974:169-71).

But even at the level of analysis used with the fourteen miracle stories, some matters were not pursued as far as they might have been. It was decided to emphasize the distinction between intervention in a positive sense (help) and intervention in a negative sense (punishment). The first seven examples illustrate the former; examples 11 to 13 have a first intervention which is negative and another following which is positive. Thus, attention was directed toward the frameworks associated with the positive and negative interventions. Other things may be done. An attempt has been made elsewhere to examine the sets of elements which can fill the various phases in the frameworks, that is, the different kinds of actors, actions, and situations which can function alone or together as problems, wrongs, and positive or negative interventions (Culley, 1975, but see the remarks to Ben-Amos in the same volume).

There remains still the question of the nature of the patterns isolated in Part III and the aim of the kind of analysis which identified them. Comments on my article in *Semeia* 3, in which these and some other patterns were introduced, asked quite directly about the nature of these patterns and their significance (Clark, Tucker). The question is valid but I would have to respond in the following terms. The immediate aim of the limited study of Part III was to use small groups of short narratives in order to bring to light the common structure shared by the group, the pattern which showed up when the stories were set side by side. It was suggested above that the results were tangible in the sense that the common structure seems to be something to be discovered in the text and not imposed from outside. That these shared patterns are significant may be seen from the fact that punishment and rescue seem to be important elements in longer and more complex narratives in biblical tradition. Furthermore, these same two subjects are frequent in the psalms and prophetic literature. The patterns in the miracle stories did not appear to be indicated by grammatical markers, although future discourse analysis may bring to light things which are not apparent now. It is not argued that these patterns are generic, either in terms of being related to social settings or in terms of being items marked and recognizable to members of the society in which they existed. In another article, some attempt was made to indicate the nature of the kind of patterns discussed above by placing them in the context of a larger aim which is concerned to delineate the anatomy of the body of tradition known as the Old Testament or Hebrew Scriptures (Culley, 1974:170). As repeated structures in this conglomerate, these patterns provide some of the coherence which holds it together as a tradition. It may not be the only way of viewing patterns like this, but it is certainly one way.

A Final Comment

While a summation was given at the end of each part, two topics of relevance to all three parts may be added briefly in this final comment. The first is on the notion of variants, a subject present in various ways throughout. In the kind of oral composition and transmission discussed in Part I, there is no concept possible of an "original" version of a given story from which all other variants derive. In a sense, the "story" may be said to consist of all its variants, a series of performances. On the other hand, the best artists produce some of the best performances of a given traditional story. Perhaps serious study of oral literature will have to include both a consideration of a traditional story as it manifests itself in a series of variants and an examination of that story as it comes to focus in an exceptionally good performance. This may be a very recent and rather striking form of the old problem of the poet against his tradition, since even in written literature no poet is entirely free from a tradition or traditions.

In biblical studies, a frequent criticism of form critics has been that they concentrate too much on the typical and ignore the individual work of genius. However this is to be resolved in the Old Testament as a whole, the stories in Part III may be a case where it is more profitable to look at a group of stories and at the common structure which the group reflects than at the individual stories, many of which are short and not particularly forceful in themselves. The force comes in the richness which results from the cumulation of several realizations of a single pattern. If there is some truth in this, there may be some possibility of applying this insight more widely to the biblical tradition with positive results.

The other comment has to do with the broad and difficult subject of oral as opposed to written literature. In discussing these two, some folklorists and students of oral literature emphasize the difference, while others see the difference as qualitative rather than quantitative. Hendricks (1970) takes the latter position and tries to relate oral to written by using the two terms "conventional" and "traditional." All literature, he argues, is

conventional but oral literature uses traditional conventions.
⟨ Written literature does not mean an absence of conventions but a
greater diversity, mixing older with new. If this distinction is valid,
then the notion of repetition in texts is important. A certain
amount and kind of repetition would indicate conventional
material and a certain amount, in this case much greater, and kind
of repetition, likely with a rather high level of similarity, would
indicate traditional material. We call texts traditional when we
recognize a lavish use of a whole range of repeated elements or, to
put it another way, a high level of redundancy within a work or
group of works (see also, Wittig, 1973). In view of the general
difficulty of establishing the precise degree to which biblical texts
are related to oral, it may be more useful to speak in terms of more
traditional and less traditional, indicating by this the relative level
of redundancy or amount of repeated elements of different kinds
found in the text. And this would include a wider range of
elements than those specifically identifiable as devices of oral
composition.

WORKS CONSULTED

Allen, Richard F.
1971

Fire and Iron: Critical Approaches to Njals Saga.
Pittsburgh: University of Pittsburgh Press.

Ben-Amos, Dan
1975

"Themes, Forms, and Meanings: Critical Comments."
Semeia 3: 128-32.

Boman, Thorlief
1967

Die Jesus-Überlieferung im Lichte der neureren Volkskunde. Göttingen: Vandenhoeck & Ruprecht.

Burney, C. F.
1970

The Book of Judges and Notes on the Hebrew Text of the Books of Kings. Reprinted with a Prolegomenon by W. F. Albright. New York: KTAV Publishing House (originally published 1918, 1903).

Childs, Brevard S.
1972

"Midrash and the Old Testament," in John Reumann, ed., *Understanding the Sacred Text.* Valley Forge: Judson Press, 45-59.

1974

The Book of Exodus. The Old Testament Library. Philadelphia: Westminster Press.

Clark, W. Malcolm
1975

"Response," *Semeia* 3: 133-36.

Coats, George W.
1968

Rebellion in the Wilderness. New York: Abingdon Press.

Crowley, Daniel J.
1966

I Could Talk Old-Story Good: Creativity in Bahamian Folklore. University of California Publications: Folklore Studies, no. 17.

Culley, Robert C.
1963

"An Approach to the Problem of Oral Tradition," *Vetus Testamentum* 13: 113-25.

1967

Oral Formulaic Language in the Biblical Psalms. Near and Middle East Series 4. Toronto: University of Toronto Press.

1974

"Structural Analysis: Is it Done with Mirrors?" *Interpretation* 28: 165-81.

1975

"Themes and Variations in Three Groups of OT Narratives," *Semeia* 3: 3-13.

Dégh, Linda
1965a

Folktales of Hungary, Translated by Judit Halasz. *Folktales of the World,* ed Richard M. Dorson. Chicago: The University of Chicago Press.

1965b

"Processes of Legend Formation," *Laographia* 22: 77-87. In German, "Prozesse der Sagenbildung," in Leander Petzoldt, ed., *Vergleichende Sagenforschung.* Darmstadt: Wissenschaftliche Buchgesellschaft. (1969)

119

1969   *Folktales and Society: Story-Telling in a Hungarian Peasant Community.* Translated by Emily M. Schossberger. Bloomington: Indiana University Press. Based on *Märchen, Erzähler und Erzählgemeinschaft.* (1962)

Finnegan, Ruth
1967   *Limba Stories and Story-Telling.* Oxford Library of African Literature. Oxford: Clarendon Press.

1970   *Oral Literature in Africa.* Oxford Library of African Literature. Oxford: Clarendon Press.

Grønbaek, Jakob H.
1971   *Die Geschichte vom Aufstieg Davids (1. Sam. 15-2 Sam. 5).* Copenhagen.

Gray, John
1970   *I & II Kings.* 2nd ed. rev. Philadelphia: The Westminster Press.

Güttgemanns, Erhardt
1971   *Offene Fragen zur Formgeschichte des Evangeliums.* Beiträge zur evangelischen Theologie 54, 2nd ed. rev. Munich: Chr. Kaiser Verlag.

1973   "Fundamentals of a Grammar of Oral Literature" A paper prepared for the IXth International Congress of Anthropological and Ethnological Sciences and soon to appear in print. The author kindly met my request for a copy.

Gunkel, Hermann
1910   *Genesis.* 3rd ed. Göttingen: Vandenhoeck & Ruprecht.

Gunn, David M.
1974   "The 'Battle Report': Oral or Scribal Convention?" *Journal of Biblical Literature* 93: 513-18.

1974   "Narrative Patterns and Oral Tradition in Judges and Samuel," *Vetus Testamentum* 24: 286-317.

Hain, Mathilde
1971   "Die Volkserzählung," *Deutsche Vierteljahrschrift für Literaturwissenschaft und Geistesgeschichte.* Sonderheft: 243-74.

Hendricks, William O.
1970   "Folklore and Structural Analysis of Literary Texts," *Language and Style* 3: 83-121.

Klemm, Hans G.
1972   "Heilige Epos und evangelische Rhapsodin," *Zeitschrift für Theologie und Kirche* 69: 1-33.

Koch, Klaus
1969   *The Growth of the Biblical Tradition.* Translated from the 2nd German ed. by S. M. Cupitt. New York: Charles Scribner's Sons.

Long, Burke O.
1973a   "2 Kings III and Genres of Prophetic Narrative," *Vetus Testamentum* 23: 337-48.

1973b   "The Effect of Divination upon Israelite Literature," *Journal of Biblical Literature* 92: 489-97.

Lord, Albert B.   "Composition by Theme in Homer and Southslavic
1951   Epos," *Transactions and Proceedings of the American
                     Philological Assocation* 82: 71-80.

1960   *Singer of Tales.* Harvard Studies in Comparative
                     Literature 24. Cambridge: Harvard University Press.

1962   "A Comparative Analysis," in Merlin Ennis, compiler and
                     translator, *Embundu: Folktales from Angola.* Boston:
                     Beacon Press.

Lüthi, Max   *Märchen,* 3rd ed. Sammlung Metzler, Realienbücher für
1967   Germanisten, Abteilung E: Poetik. Stuttgart: J. B.
                     Metzlersche Verlagsbuchhandlung.

Maranda, Pierre and Elli Köngäs Maranda, eds.
1971   *Structural Analysis of Oral Tradition.* University of
                     Pennsylvania Publications in Folklore and Folklife 3.
                     Philadelphia: University of Pennsylvania Press.

Montgomery, James A. *The Books of Kings.* Edited by Henry S. Gehman. The
1951   International Critical Commentary. Edinburgh: T. & T.
                     Clark.

Noth, Martin   *Exodus, A Commentary.* Translated by J. S. Bowden.
1962   Philadelphia: The Westminster Press. (German 1959)

Olrik, Axel   "Epic Laws of Folk Narrative," in Alan Dundes, ed., *The
1965   Study of Folklore.* Englewood Cliffs, N.J.: Prentice-Hall,
                     129-41. Originally, "Epische Gesetze der Volksdichtung,"
                     Zeitschrift für Deutsches Altertum 51 (1909): 1-12.

Ortutay, Gyula   "Principles of Oral Transmission of Folk Culture," *Acta
1959   Ethnographica* 8: 175-221.

Petersen, David L.   "A Thrice-Told Tale: Genre, Theme, and Motif," *Biblical
1973   Research* 18: 30-43.

Richter, Wolfgang   *Traditionsgeschichtliche Untersuchungen zum
1966   Richterbuch.* Bonner Biblische Beiträge 18. 2nd edition
                     revised. Bonn: Peter Hanstein Verlag.

1970   *Die sogenannten vorprophetischen Berufungsberichte.*
                     Göttingen: Vandenhoeck & Ruprecht.

Röhrich, Lutz   *Sage.* Sammlung Metzler, Realienbücher für
1965   Germanisten, Abteilung E: Poetik. Stuttgart: J. B.
                     Metzlersche Verlagsbuchhandlung.

Rofé, Alexander   "The Classification of the Prophetical Stories," *Journal of
1970   Biblical Literature* 89: 427-40.

Sandmel, Samuel   "The Haggada within Scripture," *Journal of Biblical
1961   Literature* 80: 105-22.

Scheub, Harold   "The *Ntsomi*: A Xhosa Performing Art." Unpublished
1969   Dissertation. University of Wisconsin.

1970   "The Technique of the Expansible Image in Xhosa *Ntsomi* performances," *Researches in African Literatures* 1: 119-46.

1971   "Parallel Image Sets in African Oral Narrative-Performances," *Review of National Literatures* 2: 206-23.

1972   "The Art of Nongenile Mazithathu Zenani, A Gcaleka Ntsomi Performer," in Richard M. Dorson, ed., *African Folklore*. Garden City, N.Y.: Anchor Books: 114-42.

Schmitt, Götz
1973   "Zu Gen 26:1-14," *Zeitschrift für die alttestamentliche Wissenschaft* 85: 143-56.

Scholes, Robert and Robert Kellogg
1966   *The Nature of Narrative*. New York: Oxford University Press.

Thompson, Dorothy Irving
1970?   "The Genesis Messenger Stories and Their Theological Significance: Two Methods," unpublished Doctoral Dissertation, Katholisch-Theologische Fakultät, Eberhard-Karls-Universität, Tübingen.

Tucker, Gene M.
1975   "Comments on the Articles of Robert C. Culley and Burke O. Long," *Semeia* 3: 145-48.

Van Seters, John
1972   "The Conquest of Sihon's Kingdom: A Literary Examination," *Journal of Biblical Literature* 91: 182-97.

1975   *Abraham in History and Tradition*. New Haven: Yale University Press.

Voigt, Vilmos
1972   "Some Problems of Narrative Structure Universals in Folklore," *Linguistica Biblica* 15/16: 78-90.

Wagner, Norman E.
1967   "Pentateuchal Criticism: No Clear Future," *Canadian Journal of Theology* 13: 225-32.

Westermann, Claus
1964   "Arten der Erzählung in der Genesis," *Forschung am Alten Testament*. Theologische Bücherei 24. Munich: Chr. Kaiser Verlag: 9-91.

Wittig, Susan
1973   "Formulaic Style and the Problem of Redundancy," *Centrum* 1: 123-36.

Winnett, Frederick V.
1965   "Re-examining the Foundations," *Journal of Biblical Literature* 84: 1-19.